ORIENT BLACKSWAN ANNOTATED STUDY TEXTS

William Congreve: The Way of the World

Orient BlackSwan Annotated Study Texts

The Way of the World

William Congreve

Edited by

Shirshendu Chakrabarti
Professor of English
University of Delhi

General Editor

Nissim Ezekiel

Orient BlackSwan

THE WAY OF THE WORLD

ORIENT BLACKSWAN PRIVATE LIMITED

Registered Office
3-6-752, Himayatnagar, Hyderabad 500 029, Telangana, India
e-mail: centraloffice@orientblackswan.com

Other Offices
Bengaluru, Bhopal, Chennai, Guwahati, Hyderabad, Jaipur, Kolkata, Lucknow, Mumbai, New Delhi, Noida, Patna, Visakhapatnam

First published 2007
Reprinted 2010, 2014, 2017, 2018, 2019, 2020

ISBN 978 81 250 2873 4

Typeset in 10.8/12.8 pt. Garamond

Typeset by
Bukprint
Delhi

Printed in India at
B. B. Press
Noida

Published by
Orient Blackswan Private Limited
3-6-752, Himayatnagar,
Hyderabad 500 029 (Telangana), India
e-mail: info@orientblackswan.com

CONTENTS

PREFACE

This annotated edition of *The Way of the World* by William Congreve is primarily aimed at the undergraduate and graduate student of English literature. Its strength lies in its introductory material and annotations which, the latter in particular, are either absent or kept to a minimum in the definitive editions. Before examining the play in detail, I have analysed the social and historical background and added a brief discussion of Restoration comedy, including the other comedies of Congreve.

In a similar spirit, I have ventured beyond word meanings and elucidations to comment on specific situations and contexts so that the play may come alive to the student in terms of its social, economic and intellectual milieu, its larger moorings and implications. If, in following this procedure I have imposed my own interpretation on the student, it is in the hope that the latter may be stimulated to a better understanding of the play, discovering deeper resonances and links on his or her own.

CHRONOLOGICAL TABLE

1660 The Restoration of Charles II; establishment of the Royal Society; reopening of the theatres. Daniel Defoe born.

1664 Sir John Vanbrugh born.

1665 The Great Plague.

1666 Fire of London. Molière, *The Misanthrope*.

1667 Swift born. Milton, *Paradise Lost*; Molière, *Tartuffe*

1668 Dryden, *An Essay of Dramatic Poesy*

1670 William Congreve born.

1671 Milton, *Samson Agonistes*

1672 Joseph Addison born. Richard Steele born.

1673 Moliere dead.

1674 Milton dead.

1675 Wycherley, *The Country Wife*

1676 Etherege, *The Man of Mode*

1677 Wycherley, *The Plain Dealer*

1678 The Popish Plot. Bunyan, *The Pilgrim's Progress I*; Dryden, *All for Love*. Marvell dead.

1680 Rochester, *Poems*. Rochester dead.

1681 Dryden, *Absalom and Achitophel I*

1682 Dryden, *Mac Flecknoe, Religio Laici*

1685 Charles II dead. Accession of James II. John Gay born.

1687 Newton, *Principia*

1688 The Glorious Revolution. Bunyan dead. Pope born.

1689 Accession of William III and Mary II

1690 Locke, *Essay Concerning Human Understanding*

1691 Etherege dead.

1694 Congreve, *The Double Dealer*.

1697 William Hogarth born. Vanbrugh, *The Relapse*.

1698 Jeremy Collier, *A Short View of the Immorality and Profaneness of the Stage*

1700 Dryden dead. Congreve, *The Way of the World*

1702 Accession of Queen Anne

1704 John Locke dead. Swift, *A Tale of a Tub, The Battle of the Books.*

1707 Farquhar dead. Henry Fielding born.

1709 First Copyright Act. Samuel Johnson born. Rowe's edition of Shakespeare (concluded 1710); Steele, *The Tatler* (to 1711)

1711 David Hume born. Addison, *The Spectator* (to 1712); Pope, *Essay on Criticism*

1712 Rousseau born. Pope, *Rape of the Lock* (in two Cantos); Swift, *Proposal for Correcting the English Language*

1713 Treaty of Utrecht. The Scriblerus Club. Laurence Sterne born.

1714 Accession of George I. Pope, *The Rape of the Lock* (five Cantos)

1715 Pope, *The Iliad* vol. I (completed 1720)

1716 Wycherley dead.

1719 Addison dead. Defoe, *Robinson Crusoe*

1720 South Sea Bubble

1722 Defoe, *Moll Flanders*

1725 Pope's edition of Shakespeare, *Odyssey* I-III (completed 1726; with Broome and Fenton)

1726 Vanbrugh dead. Swift, *Gulliver's Travels*

1727 Accession of George II. Newton dead. Newton, *Principia* (1st English translation)

1728 Gay, *The Beggar's Opera*; Pope, *Dunciad* (in three Books)

1729 Steele dead. Congreve dead. Edmund Burke born. Gay, *Polly, an Opera*; Swift, *A Modest Proposal*

THE AUTHOR, BACKGROUND AND AGE

William Congreve (1670-1729) was born near Leeds in Yorkshire but grew up in Ireland where his father was posted as an army officer. After studying at Kilkenny School (where Jonathan Swift had studied), he followed Swift to Trinity College, Dublin, in 1686. In preparation for a legal career, he was admitted to the Middle Temple in London in 1690, but switched to writing as he was not interested in law.

After his novel *Incognita* was published in 1692, in the following year his first comedy, *The Old Bachelor*, was staged with tremendous success. Later in the same year, his second comedy, *The Double Dealer*, had a far less enthusiastic reception perhaps because of its darker, satirical content. While these two plays were produced for the Drury Lane theatre, his remaining three plays, including the only tragedy he wrote, were for Betterton's Company in the new Lincoln's Inn Fields theatre. By returning to the usual comic conventions in *Love for Love* (1695), Congreve once again achieved popularity. His tragedy, *The Mourning Bride* (1697), was highly praised but despite its skilful use of blank verse, it has little value for literary history.

Jeremy Collier's attack on Restoration comedy rather unjustifiably picked on Congreve, who attempted a rebuttal—*Amendments of Mr. Collier's False and Imperfect Citations* (1698)—by simply noting Collier's errors and distortions. His last play, *The Way of the World* (1700), regarded by many as the finest Restoration comedy, was perhaps somewhat fine-spun for the taste of the age. The lukewarm response that it received, coupled with the tide against the comedy of manners, prompted Congreve virtually to withdraw from the stage. He was given various government posts, had many friends and no enemies and was much liked for his affable nature. Apart from his relationship with Anne Bracegirdle, the famous actress, he was later involved with Henrietta, Duchess of Marlborough.

II

The theatres which had been closed down by the Puritans reopened during the Restoration under the active guidance of Charles II.

Theatrical patents were granted to Thomas Killigrew and Sir William Davenant to set up the King's and the Duke of York's Companies respectively. Killigrew's company was housed in the Theatre Royal in Drury Lane after 1674, while Davenant's company found its home after 1671 in a new theatre in Dorset Garden. But despite the keen interest of a youthful monarch and his court, attendance at plays, after reaching a peak in the 1670s, dropped steadily. The two companies merged into the United Company in 1682, and until 1695, there was only one theatre in London. Even after 1695, until the middle of the eighteenth century, only two theatres, Drury Lane and Lincoln's Inn Fields (which became Covent Garden theatre in 1732), functioned consistently. Although decline in popularity had set in with the rise of coterie theatre in the Jacobean period itself, there were nevertheless half a dozen playhouses in London around 1600; the Restoration could not recover this situation. The physical features of the stage had also changed: instead of the apron stage with the balcony above it, we now have the proscenium arch and the front curtain. Lit by artificial light, the theatre had no place for groundlings and painted sets replaced the unadorned and unlocalised scene of Elizabethan drama.

The closing of the theatres (1642-60) during the Interregnum could not destroy histrionic talent and the Restoration dramatists were ably supported by accomplished actors like John Verbruggen, Thomas Betterton, William Bowen and Cave Underhill as well as women actors (recently introduced to the stage) like Elizabeth Barry, Mrs. Betterton and Anne Bracegirdle (the model, it is said, for Congreve's heroines). The comedy of manners did not receive similar support, however, from its audience. Play-going was dominated by the wits and hangers-on of the court for whom the play was often the occasion for a fashionable gathering not unmarked by drunken brawls. According to Pepys, the diarist, in the decade after the Restoration, apart from royal and courtly presence and patronage, the audience was composed of professional men, bureaucrats and even ordinary 'citizens'. The upper-class clientele declined after the Third Dutch War (1672-74) and the burghers began to take their place, especially in Dorset Garden Theatre, which was closer to the mercantile City than Lincoln's Inn Fields. While the burghers did not seem to mind the depiction of the merchant as a stock figure of the cuckold, their morality triumphed in the end: the unrepentant rake was increasingly replaced by the reformed rake and the stage was taken over by sentimental comedy soon after *The Way of the World* (1700).

If the comedy of manners—involving the unsentimental, witty, amoral, wry and coolly detached observation of upper-class life—is distinctive of the Restoration, Congreve remains perhaps the most elegant exponent of it. George Etherege (1635-91) may have invented the easy and sparkling prose of this sub-genre of English comedy and introduced the libertinist rake-hero on the stage. Wycherley (1640-1716) may have been more penetrating and biting in his exposure of humbug and hypocrisy and may have identified the appetite for money and power disguised as sexual licence, moral reformation and marriage. But Congreve, coming appropriately at the end of this comic tradition, provides the most subtly modulated portrayal of the entire world of polite culture delicately poised on the brink of obsolescence.

III

The Restoration of the exiled Charles II to the English throne in 1660 seemed to put an end to the Puritan Revolution and its disruptive consequences, thereby giving rise to euphoric jubilation. The Puritans had split up into many splinter groups that fought with each other and their military government as well as hypocritical corruption had made them unpopular. The Restoration itself was unusually peaceful and although the Licensing Act (1662) kept the press under a tight leash, Charles II's clemency created a sense of hope and recovery. Since the Church of England was also restored, religious extremism lost its revolutionary force; here again, despite repressive measures and continuing Nonconformist radicalism, there was a growing mood of toleration. Poets like Dryden at once saw a parallel between Restoration and the stable empire of Augustus after civil wars in Rome (31 B.C.). It became the basis for a neo-classicism cherishing the classical Roman qualities of dignity and stateliness.

But from the very beginning these values along with those of courtly wit, politeness and decorum that Charles and his coterie imported from France could not find their proper aristocratic context since the aristocracy had already been plunged into a crisis by the larger historical process of democratisation. This is the reason why the shimmering elegance and libertine gaiety of Restoration comedy are troubled by an underlying sense of emptiness. The stability restored after the Civil War was thus only a conceptual one and enthusiasm for it was short-lived.

The disrupting effect of the Financial Revolution that replaced an agrarian with the new money economy was far-reaching. The growing power of the trading classes can be seen in the energy with which London was rebuilt after the Great Fire of 1666. As the century moved towards its end, the English nobility, continuing to hold on to their country-houses, began to spend more of their time in London. Technological progress was transforming material culture making luxuries affordable for the rich. The number of hackney coaches had increased so much that legislation was required to control it. As civic amenities improved, coffee houses multiplied in number and in 1695, with the lapse of the Licensing Act, newspapers grew rapidly. Wars of commercial rivalry with Holland and France actually aided trade, giving rise to joint-stock companies and stock jobbing. The Bank of England was founded in 1694 and the Council of Trade and Plantations in 1696. The bustling, feverish excitement and startling heterogeneity of London are captured in the diaries, letters, satires, drawings and the many popular journals of the day.

The Restoration witnesses the beginning of a polarisation of court (or town) and country that would become so integral to the eighteenth century. For instance, not much later, in the Augustan periodical, *The Spectator*, (to which Addison and Steele were regular contributors) country life is presented through the eyes of the townsman 'spectator' and urban life through the eyes of the country squire, Sir Roger de Coverley. The country was commonly identified with plainness, honesty and bluff sincerity, and the town with duplicity, hypocrisy and affectation. This is the reason why the country bumpkin like Sir Wilfull (*The Way of the World*) is often introduced to the Restoration drawing room. Sir Wilfull's baffled response to the conventions of the fashionable world and his contempt for his half-brother Witwoud's pretentious *parvenu* airs put the *beau monde* in perspective, serving as a counterblast, a spontaneous and robust alternative.

If we need to see the Restoration and the eighteenth century in terms of a continuing undercurrent of de-stabilisation, we should perhaps also take a somewhat de-classicised view of the age. While classical learning no doubt held its position of importance, it was increasingly confined to the backward-looking upper classes. The centre-stage was being taken over by science and technology and the scientific temper distinguished the rising middle classes much more than the aristocracy. By 1662, the Royal Society had been established in London and its experimental research amounted to the rejection of tradition. In fact, their motto—*nullius in verba* ('on the word of no one')—is a direct challenge to the neo-classic appeal to the ancients.

As the middle classes grew in economic power, their antagonism to aristocratic culture often took the form of a moral reaction against the debauched, riotous and drunken tyranny of the Peerage, giving rise to Societies for the Reformation of Manners in the last decade of the seventeenth century. It is such a reaction that resulted in Jeremy Collier's infamous attack on Restoration Comedy of Manners, *A Short View of the Immorality and Profaneness of the English Stage* (1698). The literature that sold best in the Restoration period was predominantly religious and, whether Puritan or Anglican in persuasion, its popularity exposed the limited appeal of the literature of wit. The comedy of manners or the licentious and libertine poetry of the Earl of Rochester co-existed with the anti-aristocratic moral earnestness of *The Pilgrim's Progress* (Part I, 1678; Part II, 1684) by John Bunyan. It is this expanding chasm between the polite and popular, Cavalier and Puritan that Addison later attempts to bridge in *The Spectator* when he declares his intention 'to enliven morality with wit, and to temper wit with morality'.

The division is evident even within the genre of drama. Although the deserved fame of Congreve or Wycherley may lead us to believe that only one type of comedy, that is, comedy of manners or high comedy was prevalent, actually there were other models. Between 1660–1700, 440 new plays were produced with themes and styles ranging from the charming to the pornographic. The enclosed holiday world of high Restoration comedy needs to be re-contextualised in this revised social framework.

IV

The literature of wit, whether it is the Restoration comedy of manners or the satires of Rochester, is marked by sexual profligacy but actually there was less of sexual licence in contemporary England. Perhaps, as I shall argue later, the obsession captures the claustrophobic and inbred existence of a class outstripped by history. In other words, excluded from the bourgeois public sphere, Restoration comedy of manners was forced to confine its focus to upper class private life but it thereby turned this impoverishment into a gain, a deeper and larger social significance.

In this sub-genre of comedy, predatory sexuality invariably aims at the accumulation of property through marriage. While the sexual philandering suggests a crisis of reason, an inability to believe in stable values, the crisis finds its resolution in the acquisitive ethic of the rising middle classes. The appetite for sex and money is part of what has been called possessive individualism, a Hobbesian model of the psychology of power. Ultimately such a possessive impulse is de-humanising in its consequences, reducing human beings to mere counters of financial transaction. Marriage becomes a financial compromise between the upper and the middle classes: the economically depleted aristocracy married downwards for money while the latter married upwards for 'honour'. The obsession with adultery and cuckoldry, for which marriage is a convenient cover, fits into the bourgeois ideology of property, profit, and economic security.

The social and political writings of Locke were influential in upholding the rule of law against possessive appetite. Congreve's preoccupation with legacy conflict and contractual obligation in the context of marriage is a product of this code. In *The Way of the World*, the hero (Mirabell) and the villain (Fainall) have similar values and goals evident in their acquisitive intrigues and treatment of Mrs. Fainall. Ironically, Mirabell's triumph is that of the Restoration man of sense, the *honnete homme*, whose passions and appetites are regulated by rational calculation and who is therefore financially more successful.

V

In Restoration fashionable society, women have the freedom only of the coquette and intriguer; even their vivacious gaiety is sometimes a form of coquetry. As Millamant protests, women are free to choose their wardrobe but not their company. Imprisoned in their stagnating world of gossip centred on male sexual attention, women become malicious and mean enemies of each other in search of stability and security. The coquette represses passions precisely because they hinder and undermine the refinement of manners. However, they often break through the polished surface in unruly expressions of bitterness, spite and despair. In the hands of the finer playwrights like Etherege, Wycherley and Congreve, elegant and easy dialogue itself can become, without disrupting its smoothness and regularity, the vehicle of passions, sexual longing and love.

The cultivation of manners is not confined to women. In fact, deportment, manners and wit set the aristocrat-gentleman apart from the middle-class 'citizen' whose aspiration to nobility produced the 'bourgeois-gentleman'. University education was not enough; it needed to be supplemented by an exposure to polite manners and not unexpectedly, the emphasis fell on externalities. The middle classes often failed to acquire these traits and their false wit became a stock target of ridicule in Restoration Comedy.

The infiltration of upper-class culture by the moneyed interest—the buying and selling of peerages, for instance—which had begun in the reign of James I increased substantially under Charles I. As a result, this class began to lose authenticity and clung on to a mystique of elegant manners; the middle-class attempt to acquire this mystique gave rise to widespread affectation and hypocrisy. Suspended in a historical vacuum, the aristocracy took refuge from history in the pursuit of indolent pleasure which was nevertheless haunted by the fear of satiety. The glitter and sparkle of Restoration comedy cannot quite conceal this aimless vacuity and its modishly nihilistic philandering cloaks a fear of economic instability manifest in anxieties about marital inheritances. The conceptual and counter-historical stability that the Restoration was supposed to 'restore' is either curiously absent or problematised in the portrayal of human relationships in the comedy of manners: banished to the periphery of fashionable social life, instability returns to the centre of symbolic representation. Thus, the preoccupation with elegant manners and brilliant wit that critics have often censured for moral bankruptcy or slighted for shallow triviality is only the means to an end which is no less than a deeper fidelity to history.

RESTORATION COMEDY: A BRIEF HISTORY

The Two Phases

As far as the spirit of Restoration comedy is critical and satirical, its links with Jacobean and Caroline comedy are undeniable: dramatists like Fletcher, Shirley and Brome are among its precursors. Certainly, in a more general and pervasive way, Jacobean city comedy with its anatomy of Puritan values and bourgeois ideology provides a powerful model. Ben Jonson's comic methods and goals are endorsed in Restoration criticism, in Dryden's *Essay of Dramatic Poesy* and in Congreve's essay on humour. Apart from the conventions of English stage comedy—Shakespeare, Ben Jonson and the Jacobeans, for example––the imported model of Moliere became available to the Restoration comic dramatist.

The Restoration Comedy of Manners may have learnt the exposure of social aberration and social mobility from the French dramatist, but not his moral concern, depth and comprehensiveness. The focus in the former, as is well known, is on manners governed by the principle of decorum: every class or sub-class in society was expected to follow a pattern supposedly peculiar to it. But decorum itself is disrupted by far-reaching social transformation. This is the reason why Restoration comedy makes much of affectation, pretence and hypocrisy, using stock comic figures of the False Wit or coxcomb (Witwoud in *The Way of the World*), the fop (Sir Fopling Flutter in *The Man of Mode*), the Puritanical hypocrite or jealous husband (Heartwell and Fondlewife in *The Old Batchelor*) and of course the coy and demure woman, often ageing, disguising lust under decorous modesty (Lady Wishfort in *The Way of the World* and Lady Touchwood in *The Double Dealer*). The prevalence of 'type' characters in Restoration comedy has led critics to highlight its 'artificial' nature but surely there is an aesthetic fitness to this 'artificiality' since it enables the dramatist to hold up a faithful mirror to the social milieu and its protocols.

We may perceive two peaks in Restoration comedy, 1668-76 and 1693-1707. The contours of a comedy of manners become visible during the first period and Dryden's most successful comedy, *Marriage a la Mode* (1671), is written at this time. Critics have noted in his very first comedy, *The Wild Gallant* (1663), an early example of the Restoration gay couple (Loveby and Constance, engaged in animated verbal duel) and an anticipation of the celebrated Proviso scene of *The Way of the World* in Isabella's terms for marriage with Sir Timorous. The same crisis of reason that lies behind Rochester's poem, *Satyr Against Mankind* (1675), finds expression in the philosophy of the heroes and sometimes the heroines of the Restoration comic stage, in the cynical rejection of conventional moral values and religious beliefs. Such values were seen as Puritan hypocrisy and humbug, although the heroes promptly adopted them whenever sexual duplicity demanded it. It is, however, with Etherege that seventeenth-century libertinism acquires comic stage life. In Dorimant, libertinism reveals a feverish exultation in power over women. Although Etherege already shows his distinctive capacity for cool detachment from emotion in the dialogue of *She Wou'd if She Cou'd* (1668), his third comedy, *The Man of Mode, or Sir Fopling Flutter* (1676) remains his best. The plot is structured round the rake's progress, thereby intermeshing sexual instability with that of property and identity. Etherege also attempts to jolt Dorimant out of an ennui-ridden, aimless philandering by introducing Harriet who in turn redeems herself from the stock figure of the coquette. The play is also able to suggest the darker side to foppish affectation and the refinement of manners through occasionally vehement outbursts of emotion.

William Wycherley's first play, *Love in a Wood* (1671), may remind us of Etherege's *The Comical Revenge* (1664) in its observation of sexual intrigue across the different classes. Several characters in this play become models for future imitation: Alderman Gripe is the hypocritical Puritan, Lady Flippant is the amorous widow in search of a husband, Dapperwit is the False Wit. Everyone tries to outwit everyone else and the importance of money is evident in Dapperwit's folly: he secures Gripe's daughter for his wife but not her fortune. Unlike Etherege, Wycherley's vision is deeper and darker, for in *The Country Wife* (1675) and *The Plain Dealer* (1676) he presents a Hobbesian anatomy of the shimmering surface of Restoration society. Eschewing the detached aloofness of Etherege and Congreve, he engages in biting, sardonic ridicule of hypocrisies and affectations. The bourgeois setting of many of his plays fits in well with his distrust of aristocratic culture and the atmosphere of bitterness and malevolence suggests a moral involvement.

The indecency that had disturbed squeamish Victorian critics is actually a realistic exposure of the underbelly of the modish cult of pleasure.

In the second phase of Restoration comedy, Congreve, Vanbrugh, and Farquhar continued the spirit of the Restoration against the mounting reaction of moral censure. Jeremy Collier had mainly targeted Dryden, Wycherley, Congreve, Vanbrugh, D'Urfey, and Otway. According to him, the work of these popular dramatists encouraged immorality; added to this was their use of profanity in dialogue and hostile portrayal of clergymen. Of course, many other voices were raised against the failure of comedy to fulfil its corrective role.

Congreve's first comedy, *The Old Bachelor* (1693), to which Dryden had apparently suggested revisions, was an instant success on the stage. No doubt, the elegant wit and repartee signalled the arrival of a true successor to Etherege and Wycherley, but the dispassionate artistry of Congreve indicated a firmer control. Moreover, his deft handling of diverse stylistic registers individualised the characters. Disguise and deception predominate and the 'civilised' surface can hardly conceal the pervasive Hobbesian appetite for power through money. As Bellmour puts it clearly, Belinda (and by implication all women) are pursued as much for their wealth as for their sex appeal. Images of hunting and devouring, locate women within a context of predatory sexuality: difficulty or uncertainty of conquest offers an exciting release from boredom.

If Belinda is coquettish, affected and light-hearted, Araminta is a foil to her: she realises that male conventions of wooing reduce women to 'poor silly idols of your own making, which upon the least displeasure you forsake, and set up new.' It is this insecurity which threads the women's lives together resulting in whimsical coquetry (Belinda) and introspection (Araminta). Belinda and Araminta—the two seemingly opposed tendencies that they represent—are to find a fine amalgam later in the character of Millamant in *The Way of the World*. Millamant is the teasing coquette who keeps company with fools and is at the same time the thoughtful disputant of the proviso scene, both images hiding a lurking fear of rejection by men. Congreve's preoccupation with the link between loss of youth and intensified lust shapes the hypocritical Heartwell, a male precursor of Lady Touchwood (*The*

Double Dealer) and of course Lady Wishfort (*The Way of the World*). Heartwell's final emotional outburst also brings out the repression of passions that is part of a curious affinity between the rake and the Puritan prude. This underlying relationship in hypocrisy is skilfully portrayed later in the character of Lady Wishfort, even in her 'education' of her daughter Arabella (Mrs. Fainall).

Predatory sexuality and the ethic of unscrupulous competition acquire a distinctive, menacing edge in Congreve's next play, *The Double Dealer* (1693). Maskwell's villainy, activated by socio-economic mobility, may remind us of Iago but it certainly looks forward, especially in his partnership with Lady Touchwood, to the Fainall–Mrs. Marwood team in *The Way of the World*. The theme of warped sexual passion generating malevolence links Lady Touchwood to Mrs. Marwood, although the former, as I have mentioned above, is also a darker prefigurement of Lady Wishfort. The pursuit of and preoccupation with money is now given a familial context of legacy and posterity: the solution of the crisis plotted by the villains lies in the double contract of inheritance (Mellefont as the legitimate heir) and marriage (between Mellefont and Cynthia). In this play, Congreve ridicules the utterly trivial polite conversation that characterises the *beau monde*, invariably lapsing into false wit in their striving after polished elegance. Though reduced in scale, false wit continues to play an important role in *The Way of the World*. If Fainall and Mrs. Marwood remind us of Maskwell and Lady Touchwood, the coupling of legacy and marriage makes the situation of Mirabell and Millamant—though not much else—similar to that of Mellefont and Cynthia.

The cold public response to *The Double Dealer* turned Congreve back to conventional comedy in *Love for Love* (1695). We encounter the intertwined themes of marriage, money and inheritance: Angelica's fortune makes her a covetable prize as is evident from the hopes and schemes of Tattle and Sir Sampson. Similarly, Mrs. Frail pursues Ben entirely for the legacy that Sir Sampson plans to transfer from Valentine to him, and as soon as this possibility is obstructed, she drops him without the least hesitation. As she puts it with peeled clarity, 'marrying without an estate is like sailing in a ship without ballast' (III.i). Both Valentine, the penniless spendthrift and Angelica, the rich heiress, however, desire each other irrespective of the usual financial calculations.

When Valentine discovers that Angelica has chosen Sir Sampson for her husband—she puts on a performance matching the Hamlet-like play-acting of Valentine—he finds it futile to postpone the signing away of his inheritance. Although Angelica forestalls Valentine's disinheritance, their love is untainted by the pervasive mercenary ethic. Such love for love is somewhat unreal in the predatory greed and sexuality of Restoration upper-class society; when it is presented again, in *The Way of the World* (the love of Mirabell and Millamant), it is accommodated within the ideology of prudential calculation.

Through the characters of Miss Prue and Ben, *Love for Love* highlights the town-country opposition. If Miss Prue eagerly succumbs to urban manners and mores, Ben resists them with bluff sincerity. Here we have that delicately held equipoise, so distinctive of Congreve, whereby both town and country expose each other's shortcomings. It looks forward to Witwoud and his half-brother Sir Wilful Witwoud in *The Way of the World*: while the former aspires to and acquires a false veneer, the latter remains authentically rooted in his unpretentious robust origins.

The Critical Debate

Although contemporaries like Evelyn, Baxter or James Wright complained about the licentiousness of Restoration comedy, such criticism initially had little impact on the theatre. However, by the time Jeremy Collier wrote his *Short View of the Immorality and Profaneness of the English Stage* (1698), public opinion had changed so much that his criticism became very influential. Actually, his arguments are so flimsy and shallow that Congreve found no difficulty in rebutting them. Nevertheless, Collier's main charge that Restoration comedy does not expose vice but encourages it by rewarding vicious characters has found an echo through the centuries.

In the eighteenth century, influential critics like Addison, Steele (in *The Spectator* and *The Tatler*) and Johnson (in *Lives of the English Poets*) highlighted the undesirable effect of pleasure or elegance in alliance with vice. Such a critical climate was reinforced by the taste for sentimental, lachrymose comedy, of which Steele's *The Conscious Lovers* is a good example. Fortunately, Goldsmith's 'Essay on the Theatre' and Sheridan's plays briefly revived the traditions of Restoration comedy.

In the early nineteenth century, William Hazlitt (in *Lectures on the English Comic Writers)* and Charles Lamb ('On The Artificial Comedy of the Last Century') attempted a defence of Restoration comedy. Lamb's view that this comedy transports us to a Utopia of gallantry where profligacy cannot offend our moral sense was vehemently attacked by Macaulay ('Comic Dramatists of the Restoration'): according to the latter, Restoration comedy depicts a degraded real world and promotes an unsound morality.

It is only with the reaction against Victorianism in the early decades of the twentieth century that the rehabilitation of Restoration comedy begins. This was initiated by the efforts of critics like John Palmer, Bonamy Dobree, Joseph Wood Krutch, Kathleen M. Lynch and Virginia Woolf as well as by the popular theatrical revivals. Restoration comedy began to be read as an authentic representation of contemporary upper class society. In the late thirties, however, L.C. Knights accused it of shallowness, triviality and dullness, that is, ultimately of moral emptiness. But Knights is guilty here of the not unfamiliar confusion of means and ends: as I have argued throughout, it is precisely the wit, the preoccupation with manners, the philandering that are the means to a moral and historical critique. Recent criticism has tended to focus on the imaginative life of the comedies without losing its foothold in historical scholarship.

THE PLAY

The Action or Plot

When Congreve's *The Way of the World* was first acted in 1700 at Lincoln's Inn Fields Theatre, it was received without enthusiasm. The dramatist appears not to have been upset by the limited success, since he claims in 'To the Right Honourable Ralph, Earl of Montague, &c' that the success of the play was almost beyond his expectation, 'for but little of it was prepared for that general taste which seems now to be predominant in the palates of our audience.' Maudlin sentiment had already begun to replace elegant wit on the stage; moreover, the understated subtlety of the play may well have gone over the heads of the average Restoration audience. After the first production, the play was staged again in 1705 and despite sporadic revivals remained much less popular than *The Old Bachelor* and *Love for Love* till the twentieth century.

The other reason offered by many critics for the comparative failure of the play is its allegedly flawed structure. There is too little action in the beginning, if not throughout. But surely the specific milieu of the play—the stagnating indolence of Restoration fashionable society trapped in its inbred social circuit of the Mall or St. James's Park, of chocolate houses, gambling and cabal-nights—demands the narrowing down of action. Major characters like Millamant and Lady Wishfort are introduced late, in the second and third acts respectively. These may be important characters, but the action is controlled by the competing intrigues of two men, Mirabell and Fainall, for the conquest of the twin treasures of woman and wealth. That they appear in the opening scene should thus not surprise us, for the competing plotters, representatives of male supremacy, must be introduced to the audience before their victims or prizes are.

But what about the related view that the plot is too complicated, a tangled skein, and its effect on the audience is that of a nagging sense of confusion? At first sight, this appears to be a valid criticism. What happens in the play is so often revealed through allusion and there are so many emotional involvements complicated by family affiliations that it indeed seems difficult to keep track of the 'story'. When, in Act

I, Mirabell refers to Sir Wilfull Witwoud's relationship to Fainall, the latter's reply brings out the bewildering maze of such affiliations: 'he is half brother to this Witwoud by a former wife, who was sister to my Lady Wishfort, my wife's mother. If you marry Millamant, you must call cousins too.' (I. 167-69) We are at once given a foretaste of the enclosed world of the play. The somewhat claustrophobic nature of family-intrigue becomes the proper context for predatory greed and lust which succeed not by the force of reckless passion but by a calculating rationalistic egoism cynically disguised as worldly wisdom or 'the way of the world'. The themes of marriage, inheritance, duplicity and ennui-ridden sexual licence can intermesh in such a milieu.

Even a cursory description of what happens in the play will bring out this fragile and counter-historical structure of polished self-sufficiency. The play opens at the point when Mirabell's pursuit of Millamant under cover of feigned courtship with Lady Wishfort has suffered a setback because Mrs. Marwood, mistress to Fainall but actually in love with Mirabell, has jealously exposed the plot. Fainall's wife is Mirabell's ex-mistress, still somewhat in love with the latter and in fact, an accomplice in his further intrigues. Fainall has also suffered a setback because he had hoped to gain from the Mirabell-Millamant marriage and Mrs. Marwood's exposure has upset his financial schemes. Behind the intrigues of Mirabell and Fainall lies a typical situation involving family legacy. The presiding head, Lady Wishfort, not only controls the estate of her daughter Mrs. Fainall but also half the fortune of her niece Millamant: to inherit it the latter must marry with her aunt's approval. Since Lady Wishfort is bound to oppose the match between her niece and Mirabell, their marriage would result in her denying Millamant her share which would then go to Mrs. Fainall and thus in effect to Fainall.

Not prepared to marry Millamant without her fortune, Mirabell hatches another plot similar to the earlier one: once again Lady Wishfort's infatuation with marriage is to be exploited by feigned courtship, this time by Mirabell's servant Waitwell disguised as Sir Rowland. Mirabell takes the precaution of marrying Waitwell to Foible (Lady Wishfort's maid) so that when Lady Wishfort falls into the trap he can rescue her by producing this marriage certificate provided she in turn consents to his marriage with Millamant along with 'the moiety of her fortune'. The marriage certificate would also prevent Waitwell from turning the tables on his master. Such is Mirabell's conspiratorial skill that everybody believes in his fictitious uncle who may disinherit him by marrying Millamant or Lady Wishfort and having a child. As is bound to happen with such a load of secrecy, Mrs. Marwood chances upon Mirabell's plot and once again, it is she who exposes the intrigue and tells Fainall about Mrs. Fainall's relationship with Mirabell. On her guidance and incitement, Fainall threatens blackmail if in addition to the property of Millamant and Mrs. Fainall, Lady Wishfort's own estate is not promised to him after her death. Mirabell ultimately wins the day by virtue of the deed in which Mrs. Fainall had entrusted her property with him. The discovery of this deed in the black box is not a mechanical improbability, for it is a fitting conclusion to the sequence of secrets revealed. The Mirabell—Mrs. Fainall affair is matched by the Fainall—Mrs. Marwood one and the legal document in Fainall's possession is matched by that in the black box. The presence of false wits and the introduction of country bumpkins like Sir Wilful serve only to highlight the enclosed nature of the milieu. Appropriately, therefore, far from being loose and rambling, the plot is a tightly spun web around an inner circle of five or six diversely interlinked characters. While Mirabell sets in motion the main plot, Fainall initiates the subplot; but the two plots are so close to each other that the distinction becomes an academic one.

If the plot establishes an enclosed and inbred world, then the fragile self-sufficiency of the latter is disrupted on several levels in the play. As I have argued at length, historically the culture of elegance, wit and modish libertinism is under siege: its defences have already been breached by the inroads of nascent capitalism. The pursuit of woman is inseparable from the pursuit of a legacy. At the simplest level, the false wits like Witwoud and Petulant enable the dramatist to expose not only upstart affectation but also the meagreness of the aristocratic ideal. Congreve, it is sometimes accused, is unable to distinguish between true wit and false wit, to keep them apart. Actually, in collapsing the distance between the two, Congreve suggests the collapsing of jealously guarded class distinctions. However imperfectly, the supposedly exclusive accomplishment of wit can be imitated: upper-class speech and manners are routinely mimicked by servants and the action hinges upon the impersonation by Waitwell of a gentleman.

Themes

The intertwined themes of amorous intrigue and financial calculation are no doubt central to the play and Restoration comedy in general. Congreve locates this competitive ethic within the family ironically held together by the prospect of inheritance. In fact, inheritance is capable of controlling basic procreative instinct: not only is the Mirabell-Millamant relationship at the mercy of a legacy but even the fictitious uncle of Mirabell is a threat because he may marry, have a child and thus disinherit his nephew. These themes have already been dealt with in the introduction. Unlike Wycherley or Etherege, Congreve focuses on the possibility of love culminating in marriage. Mellefont and Cynthia (*The Double Dealer*) and Valentine and Angelica (*Love for Love*) prepare us for the mutual trust and loyalty that are emphasised in the Mirabell-Millamant relationship.

The Way of the World is on one level governed by unmitigated Hobbesian appetite that can only be controlled by law (the defeat of Fainall). If in the Proviso Scene contract means mutual trust and restraint, the final Act highlights its legal force. In fact, all the characters speak the language of law, of deeds, covenants, contracts and instruments; Congreve's legal training serves him well in this regard. There is a contract of marriage between Mirabell and Millamant, which, on Fainall's insistence, Mirabell is asked to resign. Fainall has his own covenant and of course, the original deed of conveyance in the black box solves the crisis in the end. In order to counter Fainall's machinations, even Sir Wilfull and Millamant pretend to be engaged in a contract although it 'went no farther than a little mouth-glue' and would dissolve, as Sir Wilfull warns, if Lady Wishfort does not forgive Mirabell.

The external coercion of law, however, is matched by self-imposed restraint. Thus, in the same Proviso Scene Mirabell and Millamant accept contractual adjustment and obligation as the bases for the continuance of conjugal love: these conditions make all the difference between casual sexual experience and a loving relationship. The device of the contract is a particularly happy one since it enables Congreve to suggest a new direction in marriage and gender relationship within the concepts and categories of the bourgeois ethic. Somewhat like Benedick and Beatrice in Shakespeare's *Much Ado About Nothing*, the lovers in

The Way of the World, Mirabell and Millamant, offer a critique of courtly love. For instance, Mirabell exposes Millamant's attempts to be the stereotypical cruel woman (especially in Act II) as affectation while often it is Millamant's turn to make fun of Mirabell's earnestness: 'Well, after all, there is something very moving in a love-sick face' (II. 427). At the same time, their mutual trust and affection constitute an alternative to the predatory sexuality so characteristic of upper-class Restoration society. Congreve's ironic delineation of love and marriage within a prudential ethic sets him apart from the more brutal and libertinist world of his contemporaries like Rochester, Etherege or Wycherley. His vision finds its consummation much later, perhaps in the comedy of Jane Austen.

In a sense, Restoration comedy exposes the affectation of Platonic love that had been revived as an upper-class fashion in the court of King Charles I, in the circle of Queen Henrietta, to be precise. The episode of Waitwell (disguised as the fictitious Sir Rowland) wooing Lady Wishfort, central to the action of the play, is a vigorous travesty of outdated courtly amatory rituals. In fact, we are given a list of these rituals when Lady Wishfort reveals the deceitful behaviour of Mirabell, her earlier false lover, to Waitwell, her latest false lover:

> O Sir Rowland, the hours that he has died away at my feet, the tears that he has shed, the oaths that he has sworn, the palpitations that he has felt, the trances and the tremblings, the ardours and the ecstasies, the kneelings and the risings, the heart-heavings, and the hand-grippings, the pangs and the pathetic regards of his protesting eyes!

At the same time, Mirabell's assertion to Millamant of the transforming and regenerative power of love ultimately links it to a kind of Platonism:

> You are no longer handsome when you have lost your lover; your beauty dies upon the instant. For beauty is the lover's gift; 'tis he bestows your charms, your glass is all a cheat. The ugly and the old, whom the looking glass mortifies, yet after commendation can be flattered by it, and discover beauties in it; for that reflects our praises, rather than your face.

The love that is possible and authentic in the new social order involves the fusion of instinct and reason, folly and wisdom. In the opening scene of the play, Fainall, the cynical manipulator of women and legacies, continues to pay lip service to love as the ardent idolisation of woman. Mirabell's retort highlights the co-existence of discernment and overpowering passion that is the basis for love appropriate to its milieu:

> Fainall.
>
> For a passionate lover, methinks you are a man somewhat too discerning in the failings of your mistress.
>
> Mirabell.
>
> And for a discerning man, somewhat too passionate a lover; for I like her with all her faults; nay, like her for her faults.

In the second act, where Millamant behaves whimsically with Mirabell—her behaviour is actually a disguised expression of sexual vitality—the latter is drawn to her irresistibly, but his fascination is moored in reason:

> There is no point of the compass to which they cannot turn, and by which they are not turned; and by one as well as another, for motion, not method, is their occupation. To know this, and yet continue to be in love, is to be made wise from the dictates of reason, and yet persevere to play the fool by the force of instinct.

The same act introduces us to the world of women, although in the previous act itself the reference to 'cabal-nights' had given us an inkling of the circuit of gossip, scandal and sexual liaison that imprisons them in their obsessive dependence on men. But this narrow world reveals an intensity and vulnerability of feeling that call into question the conventions of wit and elegance. Thus, men manipulate the action of the play but its soul lies in the experience of women. This experience, tied up no doubt with economic insecurity, focuses on the vagaries and disillusionments of marriage. Millamant's fear of losing her freedom in matrimony is the clearest index of marital anxieties integral to the milieu.

It is not surprising therefore that, despite their mutual distrust and barely concealed spite, Mrs. Fainall and Mrs. Marwood discuss the short-lived nature of love in the beginning of the act. For it is the fugitive nature of love and beauty that resonates poignantly at a deeper level through the play levelling down the differences among the women. Even the scheming Mrs. Marwood betrays a fit of passion in the company of Fainall and her love for Mirabell is not activated by financial calculation.

By controlling a handsome legacy, Lady Wishfort holds the reins of power but is helpless before the goading of passion. The brutal comedy of lust within a decaying body covered in heavy make-up cannot entirely hide a hint of unease. Moreover, such tragicomedy is not an isolated phenomenon but defines the very tenor of women's lives. When Mirabell sardonically remarks that Lady Wishfort would marry anything that resembled a man, Mrs. Fainall's response puts the weakness in a larger perspective: 'Female frailty! We must all come to it, if we live to be old and feel the craving of a false appetite when the true is decayed.'(II.269-71)

The fact that Mrs. Marwood, Mrs. Fainall, Lady Wishfort and Millamant all desire Mirabell is not merely indicative of his charms and accomplishments; it reduces women to competitors for the same elusive prize. Ironically, it is the similarity of fate that makes women enemies of each other. Although Mrs. Fainall does not bear any grudge against Millamant, the play does not show the kind of bonding between women that is found in Aphra Behn's *The Rover*.

Characters

Mirabell

As the man of sense, the *honnête homme* who is at the same time a mirror-image of Fainall, Mirabell exemplifies the ambiguity of the aristocratic ideal of the True-Wit. If he is the skilful manipulator of the action of the play, he is also not in full control of events. His callous and cynical treatment of Mrs. Fainall does not antagonise her even after he discards her as his mistress, and the two continue to enjoy a relationship of mutual trust. Critics who have argued that Mirabell ought to have married her himself in order to 'save that idol, reputation', tend to make the familiar confusion between character in drama and actuality. None of the characters in the play puts forward this argument and Mrs. Fainall's accusation is not that he has not married her but that he has made her marry Fainall. If Congreve wants to suggest the casual nature of the affair then its appropriateness to the milieu is evident. Perhaps the insidious affinity between Fainall and Mirabell has been overstressed, since none, not even Mrs. Marwood, his mistress-accomplice, trusts the former. Concerned as he is with polite manners and decency in front of women—witness his rebuke of Petulant's 'senseless ribaldry' (I. 470)—Mirabell nevertheless outgrows the libertinist licence of his milieu and reaches the threshold of love. His development is indicated in his sense of weariness and impatience with fashionable mores (and not merely affectation), his clear-headed, reasonable acknowledgement of an overpowering passion for Millamant and above all in his acceptance of the contractual obligations of matrimony. His preoccupation with more mundane matters of inheritance and property betrays perhaps the economic insecurity of his class but does not therefore make him a Fainall, hardened by avarice. Surely falling in love and the search for financial stability are not mutually incompatible, especially since love often needs the latter as the material basis of its survival.

Fainall

Apart from Mirabell, only Fainall among the male characters is given some depth: he is a darker version of Mirabell though ultimately not successful. Sir Wilfull Witwoud may suggest underneath his drunken rusticity a freedom from affectation and duplicity, a code of values challenging the *beau monde*, but he does not have the hardened, malevolent cynicism of Fainall. For Fainall, the love of Mirabell and Millamant is a financially lucrative prospect because if they marry they will lose their legacy which will go to his wife Mrs. Fainall. Ironically, Mrs. Marwood in her love for Mirabell ruins that prospect when she reveals to Lady Wishfort the 'plot' of Mirabell. Fainall's greed makes him an overreacher when he wants to appropriate the entire property, and leads to his downfall. Despite being a cold and calculating rationalist, he subscribes to the philosophy of the gambler and the hunter for whom the thrill of pursuit and hope is a necessary stimulus in life. He takes no relish in gambling with an indifferent Mirabell and in Act II spells out his philosophy: 'For having only that one hope, the accomplishment of it, of consequence must put an end to all my hopes;

and what a wretch is he who must survive his hopes! Nothing remains when that day comes, but to sit down and weep like Alexander, when he wanted other worlds to conquer.'(94–96)

Mrs. Marwood

As I have already argued, Mrs. Marwood is a curious mixture of cunning and unrequited passion (for Mirabell): her revelations and plots are all aimed against the marriage of Mirabell and Millamant and are therefore fuelled by jealousy. Beneath her scheming partnership with Fainall there is anger and bitterness that betray the helpless, unhappy state of women: 'It shall be all discovered. You too shall be discovered; be sure you shall. I can but be exposed. If I do it myself, I shall prevent your baseness.' (II.161–63)

Lady Wishfort

Lady Wishfort may control the coveted legacy in the play but ultimately she has no control over her life, particularly as a woman troubled by physical decay and undiminished sexual appetite. When we meet her for the first time in Act III, she is in a state of nervous anxiety about her fictitious suitor Sir Rowland, about her carefully crafted appearance, demeanour and deportment that will make an impression on him and induce him to marry her. Her face is the product of heavy make-up, and as she frowns, the cracks that become discernible in the white varnish have to be repaired. This comedy of prosthesis at once brings out the insecurity and artificial nature of women's lives in upper-class Restoration society. As Foible puts it when she is commanded to repair her face, 'a little art once made your picture like you; and now a little of the same art must make you like your picture.'(III.126–28) It is the same stranglehold of stereotypes, of life imitating art that lies behind her pastoral fantasies: 'I would retire to deserts and solitudes, and feed harmless sheep by groves and purling streams. Dear Marwood, let us leave the world, and retire by ourselves and be shepherdesses.' (V.114–17)

Lady Wishfort confesses to 'a mortal terror at the apprehension of offending against decorums' in case Sir Rowland is too shy and she is forced to be on the offensive. Life for most of the characters in the play is a matter of stylised performance, a masquerade; Lady Wishfort's obsession with it reduces it to an empty travesty. She simply cannot make up her mind if she should look coy or scornful or tender and so on. Her confusion reaches a peak in Act IV when she deliberates on the manner in which to receive her suitor. (14–28) But her decorous behaviour and affected language collapse abruptly in her angry outburst at Foible (V.1–51) In fact her abusive exuberance momentarily transports us to the world of Jacobean city comedy, to Cheapside and Smithfield Fair.

She represents the topsy-turvy meeting point of a dying order and emergent bourgeois ideology, of voracious sexual appetite and Puritan piety. The books she displays in her collection and the education she claims to have given to her daughter are both heavily, somewhat absurdly, biased in favour of Puritan morality. Beset with the anxieties of old age and physical decay, she deceives herself about her physical charm: even her niece Millamant is not pretty enough to copy her look of tenderness, 'a sort of dyingness', 'a swimmingness in the eyes.' (III.139–42) Self-deception prompts her to deception and the disguise of sanctimonious hypocrisy. She betrays her geriatric lust in protesting too much about her purity and innocence to Sir Rowland/Waitwell: 'Sir Rowland, you must not attribute my yielding to any sinister appetite, or indigestion of widowhood; nor impute my complacency to any lethargy of continence. I hope you do not think me prone to any iteration of nuptials.' (IV.454–57) When she claims to be free from 'the least scruple of carnality', the undeceived Waitwell affirms tongue in cheek: 'You are all camphire and frankincense, all chastity and odour.' (IV.468–69)

Mrs. Fainall

Although she is ill-treated by both Fainall and Mirabell, Mrs. Fainall remains unusually dignified and not really a passive victim; even her hateful marriage does not make her bitter or mean. Her loyalty to Mirabell invites the open admiration of Foible: 'O dear madam, Mr. Mirabell is such a sweet, winning gentleman, but your ladyship is the pattern of generosity. Sweet lady, to be so good!' (III.167–69) Her generosity is largely unrecognised, however, and Mrs. Marwood is cynical enough to suggest in the same scene that she is carrying on a clandestine affair with Mirabell and procuring women for him. If the world ignores her merits, if she stands a little aloof from the action, then her potential as a critic of society is not developed in the play. Of course, Congreve may not have been interested in this potential but Mrs. Fainall's presence makes us feel morally uncomfortable about the position of women in society.

Millamant

The very first reference to Millamant is to her whimsical temperament, to her 'humours that would tempt the patience of a stoic.'(I.17-18) Later in the act, we discover 'that it is almost a fashion to admire her', but despite her beauty, Witwoud will never break his heart for her because 'she's a sort of an uncertain woman.'(I.398–403) Mirabell himself is bewildered by the variety of her disposition.

Unlike the others, however, he discerns through the coquettish pose an ebullient vitality and is irresistibly drawn to it. After her bustling entry in the second act, we may sense a link between her moody, whimsical manner and love for Mirabell; even in the next act, this link is discernible in her somewhat sentimental wish to have music to keep up her spirits, a song agreeable to her 'humour'. Appropriately enough, when she claims that she loves to give pain, it is Mirabell who calls her bluff: 'You would affect a cruelty which is not in your nature; your true vanity is in the power of pleasing.'(II.334–35) Her beauty and vitality are moored in the discovery of a loving relationship and in this sense is the lover's gift.

If Mirabell's sententiousness and proprietorial air indicate love, in the case of Millamant it is her playful teasing of Mirabell. She flaunts her trust in and power over Mirabell before Mrs. Marwood, not without a touch of feminine malice: 'Poor Mirabell! His constancy to me has quite destroyed his complaisance for all the world beside.'(III.283–85) Her seemingly flippant manner with Mirabell is thus the very mode in which her sexual vitality and joyousness bubble forth: this is the way passion puts on the disguise of wit in Restoration comedy.

Millamant's moodiness also indicates boredom and dissatisfaction with a milieu that is particularly oppressive to a woman with a mind of her own. Surrounded by fools, false wits and hypocrites, she laments the lot of women, free to choose their clothes but not their company. If love offers a mode of escape, it carries within it the constant threat of deception or disenchantment; in actuality, it is often casual sexual intrigue. Marriage may be the inevitable goal of all women, but the hypocrisy and servitude that it promises also make it the chief source of their anxiety. Even after the Proviso Scene Millamant is not sure of her rights after marriage: 'Well, if Mirabell should not make a good husband, I am a lost thing—for I find I love him violently.' (IV.273–74)

THE PROVISO SCENE

The Proviso or Bargain Scene in Act IV has received critical attention because of the marital contract between Mirabell and Millamant which suggests the possibility of equality in love and marriage within the framework of bourgeois society. The scene may be said to begin when Sir Wilful leaves the company of Millamant and Mirabell enters, completing the couplet from Edmund Waller that Millamant had begun to recite. At once, a bond is set up between the two lovers. When Mirabell asks if his pursuit of her love is now to be crowned with success, Millamant desires never to be freed from pursuit, 'from the agreeable fatigues of solicitation', not even after marriage. Actually, Millamant's abstracted moodiness in the entire act proceeds from her approaching marriage with Mirabell, which puts her in a quandary. Marriage in her milieu is a financial arrangement and even if it is the culmination of love for her, prudential calculation must play a part in it. Mirabell and Millamant cannot marry without Lady Wishfort's legacy.

But the financial ethic is redeemed of its unscrupulous potential by the concept of contract, of bargain and exchange which Congreve transfers from the public sphere to the intimate and domestic. The lovers bargain over conjugal rights and duties in a spirit of give and take, looking forward, however unsatisfactorily, to the future. In the process, Millamant and Mirabell question the codes of hypocrisy and affectation that permeate the amatory and marital conventions of their world. Millamant is apprehensive of losing her liberty and therefore wishes to demarcate a private space within the routine of domestic life (183–195). This unusual demand is matched in the public space by a systematic eschewal of the insincere fashions of conjugal behaviour (165–80). She will not be called names 'as wife, spouse, my dear, joy, jewel, love, sweetheart, and the rest of that nauseous cant, in which men and their wives are so fulsomely familiar.' She refuses to be 'familiar or fond', to 'kiss before folks', to 'go to Hyde Park together the first Sunday in a new chariot, to provoke eyes and whispers; and then never to be seen there together again', and so on. What is common to these conditions, public and private, is the characteristic amalgam of levity and seriousness: Millamant's demands make us aware of the woman's need for honesty and freedom in domestic life without making us forget the codes of effervescent wit and flippancy.

If Millamant reconciles herself to dwindle by degrees into a wife, Mirabell similarly desires not to be enlarged beyond measure into a husband. Accordingly, he demands that Millamant should move out of the enclosed and trivial world of intrigue and fashion that is reserved for women. She must not have a female confidante or be escorted by a fop to the playhouse in a mask. She must free herself from the common obsession with beauty aids and slimming techniques which interfere with child-bearing and thus suppress the fundamental procreative instinct. Like Millamant's provisos, Mirabell's also look beyond upper-class Retoration society and at the same time authentically grow out of it: Mirabell's love is not free from the proprietorial tone of the Restoration husband.

We encounter this authenticity above all in Congreve's use of wit and repartee in the play, particularly in the Proviso Scene. Wit becomes the specific, the historically appropriate garb in which feeling and passion may find expression in the milieu of modish sophistication. The sober language of bargain and exchange is enlivened by an ebullient wit that is gratuitous, not intrinsic to the sobriety. Congreve's wit (and perhaps all wit in Restoration theatre) has in other words a sub-text of emotion, the intensity of which is directly proportional to the elegance of the former.

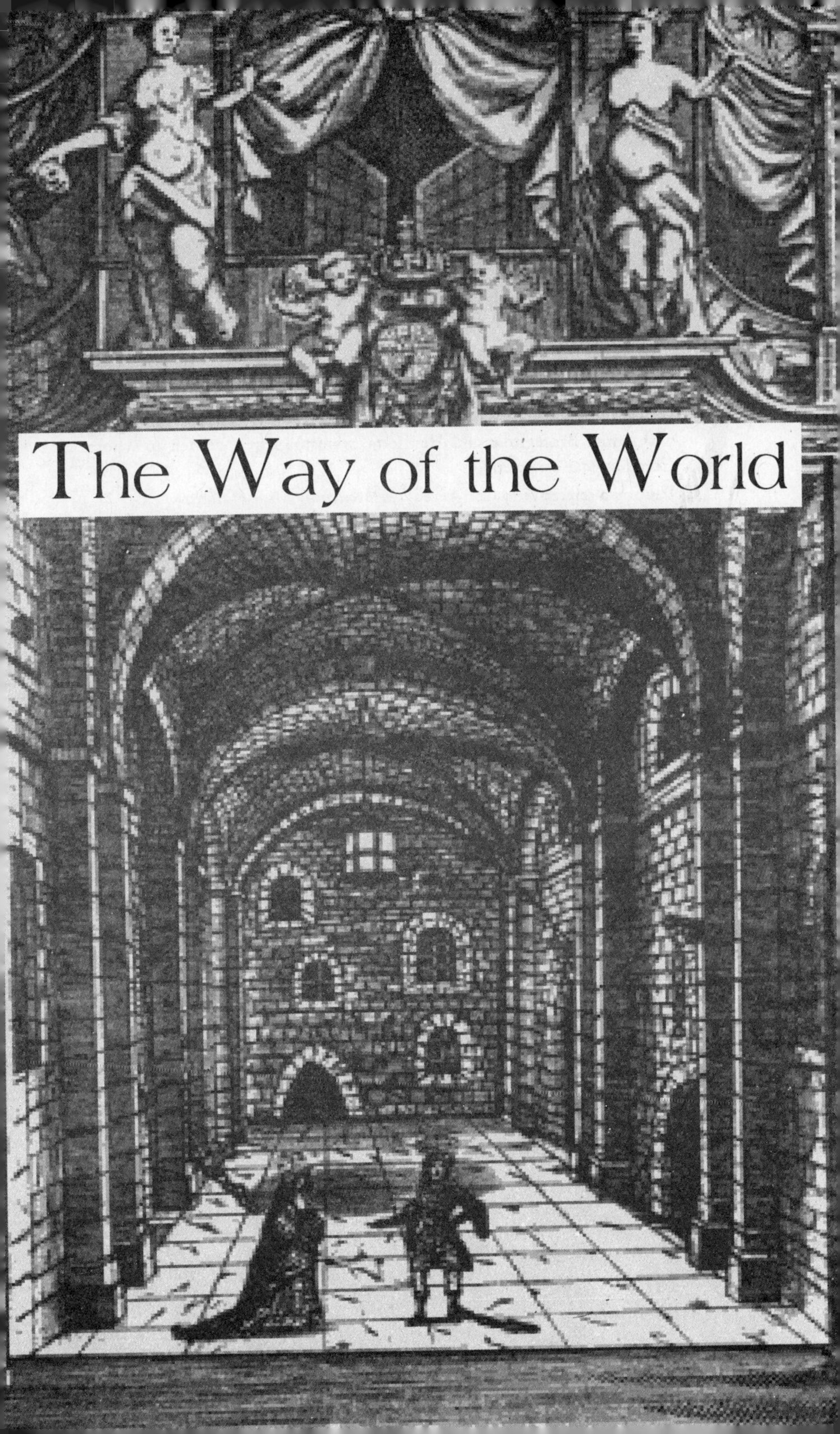
The Way of the World

7 nice: fastidious, refined

10 awful: awe-inspiring

12 quaff: drink a large amount at one go

15 Arabella: Arabella Hunt, the beautiful singer and lutanist, for whom the young Congreve wrote his ode *Upon a Lady's Singing* (1692). She, along with Anne Bracegirdle and Henrietta, were the three women to whom Congreve was attracted.

19 Pastora: a reference to Congreve's *The Mourning Muse of Alexis*.

23 William: William III, King of England, Scotland & Ireland (1689–1702)

COMMENDATORY VERSES

To Mr. Congreve, occasioned by his Comedy called "The Way of the World."

When pleasure's falling to the low delight,
In the vain joys of the uncertain sight;
No sense of wit when rude spectators know,
But in distorted gesture, farce and show;
How could, great author, your aspiring mind
Dare to write only to the few refined?
Yet though that nice ambition you pursue,
'Tis not in Congreve's power to please but few.
Implicitly devoted to his fame,
Well-dressed barbarians know his awful name;
Though senseless they're of mirth, but when they laugh,
As they feel wine, but when, till drunk, they quaff.
On you from fate a lavish portion fell
In every way of writing to excel.
Your muse applause to Arabella brings,
In notes as sweet as Arabella sings.
Whene'er you draw an undissembled woe,
With sweet distress your rural numbers flow;
Pastora's the complaint of every swain,
Pastora still the echo of the plain!
Or if your muse describe, with warming force,
The wounded Frenchman falling from his horse;
And her own William glorious in the strife,
Bestowing on the prostrate foe his life;
You the great act as generously rehearse,
And all the English fury's in your verse.
By your selected scenes and handsome choice;
Ennobled Comedy exalts her voice;
You check unjust esteem and fond desire,
And teach to scorn what else we should admire;
The just impression taught by you we bear,
The player acts the world, the world the player,
Whom still that world unjustly disesteems,

40 mask: put on a mask in order to go to the theatre
41 Mourning Bride: Congreve's tragedy, *The Mourning Bride* (1697)
51 R. Steele: Sir Richard Steele (1672–1729), essayist and dramatist

Though he alone professes what he seems.
But when your muse assumes her tragic part,
She conquers and she reigns in every heart;
To mourn with her men cheat their private woe,
And generous pity's all the grief they know.
The widow, who, impatient of delay,
From the town joys must mask it to the play,
Joins with your Mourning Bride's resistless moan,
And weeps a loss she slighted, when her own;
You give us torment, and you give us ease,
And vary our afflictions as you please,
Is not a heart so kind as yours in pain,
To load your friends with cares you only feign;
Your friends in grief, composed yourself, to leave?
But 'tis the only way you'll e'er deceive.
Then still, great sir, your moving power employ,
To lull our sorrow and correct our joy.

R. STEELE

2 arraign: accuse

7 prefer: proffer

15–17 Since the play enjoyed only moderate success on the stage, Congreve seems to confirm Steele's opinion (in 'Commendatory Verses') that he wrote against the grain of popular taste

18ff Rejecting gross or natural folly as a comic target, Congreve focuses on hypocrisy and affectation, particularly the phenomenon of false wit, which becomes difficult to distinguish from the true in a context of social mobility

TO THE RIGHT HONOURABLE RALPH, EARL OF MONTAGUE, &c.

My Lord,

Whether the world will arraign me of vanity or not, that I have presumed to dedicate this comedy to your Lordship, I am yet in doubt, though it may be it is some degree of vanity even to doubt of it. One who has at any time had the honour of your Lordship's conversation, cannot be supposed to think very meanly of that which he would prefer to your perusal; yet it were to incur the imputation of too much sufficiency, to pretend to such a merit as might abide the test of your Lordship's censure.

Whatever value may be wanting to this play while yet it is mine, will be sufficiently made up to it when it is once become your Lordship's; and it is my security that I cannot have overrated it more by my dedication than your Lordship will dignify it by your patronage.

That it succeeded on the stage was almost beyond my expectation; for but little of it was prepared for that general taste which seems now to be predominant in the palates of our audience.

Those characters which are meant to be ridiculous in most of our comedies are of fools so gross that, in my humble opinion, they should rather disturb than divert the well-natured and reflecting part of an audience; they are rather objects of charity than contempt; and instead of moving our mirth, they ought very often to excite our compassion.

This reflection moved me to design some characters which should appear ridiculous, not so much through a natural folly (which is incorrigible, and therefore not proper for the stage) as through an affected wit; a wit, which, at the same time that it is affected, is also false. As there is some difficulty in the formation of a character of this nature, so there is some hazard which attends the progress of its success upon the stage; for many come to a play so over-charged with criticism that they very often let fly their censure, when through their rashness they have mistaken their aim. This I had occasion lately to observe; for this play had been acted two or three days before some of these hasty judges

44ff The familiar theme of the petty professional writer, the Grub Street hack in Swift's *A Tale of a Tub* or Pope's *The Dunciad*, debasing literary and therefore cultural standards.
45 Terence: Roman comic dramatist (ca 195–159B.C.)
45–46 Scipio ...Laelius: Scipio Africanus and Caius Laelius, patrons of Terence
52 Plautus: Roman comic dramatist (ca. 254–184B.C.)
52 Horace: great poet of Augustan Rome (65–8B.C.) and arbiter of taste (Cf. his *Ars Poetica*)
56 fable: plot
59 Menander: the most famous writer of New Comedy in Greece
62–63 Theophrastus: Greek writer, whose characters served as a model for seventeenth century 'character writing'
68ff Polite conversation, brilliantly satirised by Swift (*Polite Conversation*), was nevertheless the basis for a neo-classical aesthetic in England

could find the leisure to distinguish betwixt the character of a Witwoud and a Truewit.

I must beg your Lordship's pardon for this digression from the true course of this epistle; but that it may not seem altogether impertinent, I beg that I may plead the occasion of it, in part of that excuse of which I stand in need, for recommending this comedy to your protection. It is only by the countenance of your Lordship, and the *few* so qualified, that such who write with care and pains can hope to be distinguished; for the prostituted name of *poet* promiscuously levels all that bear it.

Terence, the most correct writer in the world, had a Scipio and a Laelius, if not to assist him, at least to support him in his reputation; and notwithstanding his extraordinary merit, it may be their countenance was not more than necessary.

The purity of his style, the delicacy of his turns, and the justness of his characters were all of them beauties which the greater part of his audience were incapable of tasting; some of the coarsest strokes of Plautus, so severely censured by Horace, were more likely to affect the multitude, such who come with expectation to laugh out the last act of a play, and are better entertained with two or three unseasonable jests than with the artful solution of the *fable*.

As Terence excelled in his performances, so had he great advantages to encourage his undertakings, for he built most on the foundations of Menander; his plots were generally modelled, and his characters ready drawn to his hand. He copied Menander, and Menander had no less light in the formation of his characters from the observations of Theophrastus, of whom he was a disciple; and Theophrastus, it is known, was not only the disciple, but the immediate successor of Aristotle, the first and greatest judge of poetry. These were great models to design by; and the further advantage which Terence possessed, towards giving his plays the due ornaments of purity of style and justness of manners, was not less considerable from the freedom of conversation which was permitted him with Laelius and Scipio, two of the greatest and most polite men of his age. And indeed the privilege of such a conversation is the only certain means of attaining to the perfection of dialogue.

74 correct: Congreve reiterates the neo-classical aesthetic of 'correctness' or decorum which emphasised regularity, refinement and urbanity.

77 conversation: Sober and elegant conversation, as opposed to polemic and controversy, is directly made the basis of Congreve's Restoration comedy.

88 The eldest sister: A reference to the place of privilege given from Aristotle onwards to poetry over the sister arts of painting, music and so on.

If it has happened in any part of this comedy that I have gained a turn of style or expression more correct, or at least more corrigible, than in those which I have formerly written, I must, with equal pride and gratitude, ascribe it to the honour of your Lordship's admitting me into your conversation, and that of a society where everybody else was so well worthy of you, in your retirement last summer from the town; for it was immediately after that this comedy was written. If I have failed in my performance, it is only to be regretted, where there were so many not inferior either to a Scipio or a Laelius, that there should be one wanting equal to the capacity of a Terence.

If I am not mistaken, poetry is almost the only art which has not yet laid claim to your Lordship's patronage. Architecture and painting, to the great honour of our country, have flourished under your influence and protection. In the meantime, poetry, the eldest sister of all arts, and parent of most, seems to have resigned her birthright, by having neglected to pay her duty to your Lordship, and by permitting others of later extraction to prepossess that place in your esteem to which none can pretend a better title. Poetry, in its nature, is sacred to the good and great; the relation between them is reciprocal, and they are ever propitious to it. It is the privilege of poetry to address to them, and it is their prerogative alone to give it protection.

This received maxim is a general apology for all writers who consecrate their labours to great men; but I could wish at this time that this address were exempted from the common pretence of all dedications; and that, as I can distinguish your Lordship even among the most deserving, so this offering might become remarkable by some particular instance of respect, which should assure your Lordship that I am, with all due sense of your extreme worthiness and humanity,

My Lord,
Your Lordship's most obedient
and most obliged humble servant
WILL. CONGREVE

Despite its light-hearted tone, the Prologue senses the uncertainties beginning to be faced by writers. Mr Betterton was a famous Restoration actor.

7 cuckoo eggs: the cuckoo lays its eggs in the nests of other birds

8 changeling: Child substituted for another by stealth.

11 bubbles: fools

20 *Parnassus:* sacred mountain-abode of the Muses

25 dullness: Dryden in 'Mac Flecknoe' head virtually begun the satire on literacy-cultural dullness developed by Swift (*A Tale of a Tub*) and Pope (*The Dunciad*).

PROLOGUE

Spoken by Mr. Betterton

Of those few fools, who with ill stars are cursed,
Sure scribbling fools, called poets, fare the worst;
For they're a sort of fools which Fortune makes,
And after she has made 'em fools, forsakes.
With Nature's oaf 'tis quite a different case,
For Fortune favours all her idiot race;
In her own nest the cuckoo eggs we find,
O'er which she broods to hatch the changeling kind.
No portion for her own she has to spare,
So much she dotes on her adopted care.
 Poets are bubbles, by the town drawn in,
Suffered at first some trifling stakes to win;
But what unequal hazards do they run!
Each time they write they venture all they've won;
The squire that's buttered still is sure to be undone.
This author, heretofore, has found your favour,
But pleads no merit from his past behaviour.
To build on that might prove a vain presumption,
Should grants to poets made admit resumption;
And in Parnassus he must lose his seat
If that be found a forfeited estate.
 He owns, with toil he wrote the following scenes,
But if they're naught ne'er spare him for his pains.
Damn him the more; have no commiseration
For dullness on mature deliberation.
He swears he'll not resent one hissed-off scene,
Nor, like those peevish wits, his play maintain,
Who, to assert their sense, your taste arraign.
Some plot we think he has, and some new thought,
Some humour too, no farce—but that's a fault.
Satire, he thinks, you ought not to expect;
For so reformed a town who dares correct?
To please this time has been his sole pretence;
He'll not instruct, lest it should give offence.
Should he by chance a knave or fool expose

36 That hurts none here: Congreve's comic vision is unique in its eschewal of coarseness and delicate modulation of the darker elements. This remains an important difference with contemporaries like Etherege and Wycherley.

That hurts none here; sure here are none of those.
In short, our play shall (with your leave to show it)
Give you one instance of a passive poet,
Who to your judgments yields all resignation;
So save or damn, after your own discretion.

DRAMATIS PERSONAE

Men

FAINALL, in love with MRS. MARWOOD	MR. BETTERTON
MIRABELL, in love with MRS. MILLAMANT	MR. VERBRUGGEN
WITWOUD, Followers of MRS. MILLAMANT	MR. BOWEN
PETULANT, Followers of MRS. MILLAMANT	MR. BOWMAN
SIR WILFULL WITWOUD, Half-brother to WITWOUD, and NEPHEW to LADY WISHFORT	MR. UNDERHILL
WAITWELL, Servant to MIRABELL	MR. BRIGHT

Women

LADY WISHFORT, Enemy to MIRABELL, for having falsely pretended love to her	MRS. LEIGH
MRS. MILLAMANT, A fine lady, Niece to LADY WISHFORT, and loves MIRABELL	MRS. BRACEGIRDLE
MRS. MARWOOD, Friend to MR. FAINALL, and likes MIRABELL	MRS. BARRY
MRS. FAINALL, Daughter to LADY WISHFORT, and Wife to FAINALL, formely Friend to MIRABELL	MRS. BOWMAN
FOIBLE, Woman to LADY WISHFORT	MRS. WILLIS
MINCING, WOMAN TO MRS. MILLAMANT	MRS. PRINCE

Dancers, Footmen, and Attendants

SCENE—LONDON

The time equal to that of the presentation.

[I] A Chocolate-house: The model for this is probably White's Chocolate House, established in St. James's Street (1699). Since this was a fashionable meeting-place for upper-class gentlemen of leisure, it provides an appropriate opening locale for the play. Chocolate like coffee had become a popular drink among this class of people, having been recently introduced in the West because of the expansion of colonial trade.

2 done: finished the game of cards

6 gamester: gambler

6–9 the coldness ... reputation: an instance of typical Restoration wit reducing life to a mere sport. Notice how the balanced expression suggests through the modish profligacy a view of life as a never-ending game. The upper-class passion for gambling betrays the uncertainty and instability of that class in an emerging capitalist society.

10–11 The delicate taste suggests an over-refined, jaded sensibility characteristic of the social context of Restoration comedy.

12–13 humours: whimsical moods. Ben Jonson introduced the term in literature in his comedy of Humours. The word was derived from medieval medicine. According to it, the human body consisted of four chief fluids, blood, phlegm, choler and black choler. The proportion of each fluid in the body determined the person's character.

18 stoic: person of great self-control indifferent to pleasure and pain. Originally meant a follower of the philosophical sect founded by Zeno c.308 B.C. at Athens.

coxcomb: conceited showy person. Coxcomb = cock's comb, which originally referred to the cap worn by a professional fool. Millamant enjoys teasing Mirabell by encouraging or tolerating such fools.

The Way of the World
A Comedy

A Chocolate-house

Act I, Scene I

Mirabell *and* Fainall, *rising from cards*; Betty *waiting*

MIRABELL.

You are a fortunate man, Mr. Fainall.

FAINALL.

Have we done?

MIRABELL.

What you please. I'll play on to entertain you.

FAINALL.

No, I'll give you your revenge another time; when you are not so indifferent; you are thinking of something else now, and play too negligently. The coldness of a losing gamester lessens the pleasure of the winner. I'd no more play with a man that slighted his ill fortune than I'd make love to a woman who undervalued the loss of her reputation.

MIRABELL.

You have taste extremely delicate and are for refining on your pleasures.

FAINALL.

Prithee, why so reserved? Something has put you out of humour.

MIRABELL.

Not at all; I happen to be grave today, and you are gay; that's all.

FAINALL.

Confess, Millamant and you quarrelled last night, after I left you; my fair cousin has some humours that would tempt the patience of a stoic. What, some coxcomb came in, and was well received by her, while you were by.

21 genius: guardian spirit

23 Lady Wishfort's passion for Mirabell, rebuffed by the latter, is now laced with hatred and resentment. The figure of the old widow or spinster desiring the attention of young men is a telling comment on the stifling indolence, boredom and drabness in the life of upper-class women. Anticipated in other plays of Congreve, the prototype of Lady Wishfort is perhaps Lady Flippant in Wycherley's first play, *Love in a Wood* (1671). Her passion is an important element in the action since Mirabell's plans are all aimed at neutralising her hostility.

24ff the world of women

27 vapours: hypochondria or depression, a fashionable malady of the women in the seventeenth century

31 taciturnity: unwillingness to speak

31 invective: violent, abusive attack in words

39–42 As Mirabell refers to Millamant's mental independence of her aunt, Fainall reminds him of her economic dependence on her: sexual love, marriage and property or inheritance are interwoven strands in the play.

41 fortune: Millamant's fortune of twelve thousand pounds is rather large.

MIRABELL.

Witwoud and Petulant, and what was worse, her aunt, your wife's mother, my evil genius; or to sum up all in her own name, my old Lady Wishfort came in.

FAINALL.

Oh, there it is then! She has a lasting passion for you, and with reason. What, then my wife was there?

MIRABELL.

Yes, and Mrs. Marwood and three or four more, whom I never saw before. Seeing me, they all put on their grave faces, whispered one another; then complained aloud of the vapours, and after fell into a profound silence.

FAINALL.

They had a mind to be rid of you.

MIRABELL.

For which reason I resolved not to stir. At last the good old lady broke through her painful taciturnity, with an invective against long visits. I would not have understood her, but Millamant joining in the argument, I rose and with a constrained smile told her, I thought nothing was so easy as to know when a visit began to be troublesome. She reddened and I withdrew, without expecting her reply.

FAINALL.

You were to blame to resent what she spoke only in compliance with her aunt.

MIRABELL.

She is more mistress of herself than to be under the necessity of such a resignation.

FAINALL.

What? though half her fortune depends upon her marrying with my lady's approbation?

MIRABELL.

I was then in such a humour, that I should have been better pleased if she had been less discreet.

46 cabal-nights: evening gatherings at which women engaged in secret intrigue (cabal) and gossip. The parallel with political intrigue is comic while the enclosed world of female gossip suggests a prison within the prison of upper-class life.

48 coroner's inquest: inquiry held by officer as to the cause of any violent or unnatural death; here used wittily about the 'murdered reputations'

53 Witwoud and Petulant: 'coxcombs' whose folly made them eligible for membership of the cabal of women

57 ratafia: a drink flavoured with almonds or kernels of fruits
shift: take care

58 sham addresses: false courtship or courteous advances

64ff Perhaps there is a suggestion here of the growing helplessness of Lady Wishfort's situation. Without beauty and sexual attraction, so crucial to the life of upper-class women, there is nothing left in her ennui-ridden life. Despite her folly, meanness and lust, it is tempting to see the shade of a deceived victim in her character.

65 lampoon: abusive satire attacking an individual, here Lady Wishfort.

66 imputation: attributing or ascribing to someone

68 dropsy: disease in which watery fluid collects in cavities or tissues of the body and swells it up.

71 debauch: seduce

FAINALL.

Now I remember, I wonder not they were weary of you. Last night was one of their cabal-nights; they have 'em three times a week, and meet by turns, at one another's apartments, where they come together like the coroner's inquest, to sit upon the murdered reputations of the week. You and I are excluded; and it was once proposed that all the male sex should be excepted; but somebody moved that, to avoid scandal, there might be one man of the community; upon which motion Witwoud and Petulant were enrolled members.

MIRABELL.

And who may have been the foundress of this sect? My Lady Wishfort, I warrant, who publishes her detestation of mankind, and full of the vigour of fifty-five, declares for a friend and ratafia; and let posterity shift for itself, she'll breed no more.

FAINALL.

The discovery of your sham addresses to her, to conceal your love to her niece, has provoked this separation. Had you dissembled better, things might have continued in the state of nature.

MIRABELL.

I did as much as man could, with any reasonable conscience. I proceeded to the very last act of flattery with her, and was guilty of a song in her commendation. Nay, I got a friend to put her into a lampoon, and compliment her with the imputation of an affair with a young fellow, which I carried so far, that I told her the malicious town took notice that she was grown fat of a sudden; and when she lay in of a dropsy, persuaded her she was reported to be in labour. The devil's in't, if an old woman is to be flattered further, unless a man should endeavour downright personally to debauch her; and that my virtue forbade me. But for the discovery of that amour, I am indebted to your friend, or your wife's friend, Mrs. Marwood.

84 tender: considerate
84–89 An example of witty circumlocution in which each accuses the other of a secret involvement with Mrs Marwood.
88 confesses: shows or reveals that
90 censorious: disapproving
95 last canonical hour: noon. Canonical hours were from eight to twelve noon during which marriages could be legally performed in church.
96 jade: woman (colloquial and jocular)

FAINALL.

What should provoke her to be your enemy, unless she has made you advances, which you have slighted? Women do not easily forgive omissions of that nature.

MIRABELL.

She was always civil to me, till of late. I confess I am not one of those coxcombs who are apt to interpret a woman's good manners to her prejudice, and think that she who does not refuse 'em everything can refuse 'em nothing.

FAINALL.

You are a gallant man, Mirabell; and though you may have cruelty enough not to satisfy a lady's longing, you have too much generosity not to be tender of her honour. Yet you speak with an indifference which seems to be affected, and confesses you are conscious of a negligence.

MIRABELL.

You pursue the argument with a distrust that seems to be unaffected, and confesses you are conscious of a concern for which the lady is more indebted to you than your wife.

FAINALL.

Fie, fie, friend! If you grow censorious, I must leave you. I'll look upon the gamesters in the next room.

MIRABELL.

Who are they?

FAINALL.

Petulant and Witwoud. [*To* Betty.] Bring me some chocolate.

Exit.

MIRABELL.

Betty, what says your clock?

BETTY.

Turned of the last canonical hour, sir. *Exit.*

MIRABELL.

How pertinently the jade answers me! [*Looking on his watch.*] Ha? almost one o'clock! Oh, y'are come!

98ff Upper-class Restoration society continues to rely on the loyalty and cooperation of servants: in this play they play a crucial role behind the success of Mirabell's plot and exposure of Fainall. Moreover, the servant's speech seems to offer an alternative undisguised sexuality and fertility-worship to the veiled and sterile version predominant in the *beau monde*. Waitwell's impersonation of the fictitious Sir Rowland is not merely an element of the plot and action, but is a comment on the increasing devaluation of aristocratic culture in a context of social mobility.

98 something tedious: rather slow

99 coupling: marriage

Pancras: St. Pancras Church where licences were not necessary for marriage.

100 country dance: any rural English dance in which couples often stood face to face in two long lines

101 dispatch: prompt settlement

102 parson: vicar or any beneficed clergyman

104 Duke's Place: St. James's Church where also licences were not necessary for marriages.

104 in a trice: in a moment, instantly

110 liveries: distinctive dress worn by servants and officers.

112–113 adjourn the consummation: This refers to the marriage and its consummation.

113–114 shake his ears: like a dog

Dame Partlet: Pertelote, the hen, wife of Chauntecleer in the beast fable used by Chaucer in *The Nun's Priest's Tale*.

115 Rosamond's Pond: a little lake in St. James's Park, frequented by lovers

116 tender: care for

Enter a Servant.

Well, is the grand affair over? You have been something tedious.

SERVANT.

Sir, there's such coupling at Pancras, that they stand behind one another, as 'twere in a country dance. Ours was the last couple to lead up; and no hopes appearing of dispatch, besides the parson growing hoarse, we were afraid his lungs would have failed before it came to our turn; so we drove round to Duke's Place, and there they were riveted in a trice.

MIRABELL.

So, so, you are sure they are married.

SERVANT.

Married and bedded, sir; I am witness.

MIRABELL.

Have you the certificate?

SERVANT.

Here it is, sir.

MIRABELL.

Has the tailor brought Waitwell's clothes home, and the new liveries?

SERVANT.

Yes, sir.

MIRABELL.

That's well. Do you go home again, d'ye hear, and adjourn the consummation till farther order; bid Waitwell shake his ears, and Dame Partlet rustle up her feathers, and meet me at one o'clock by Rosamond's Pond, that I may see her before she returns to her lady; and as you tender your ears, be secret.

Exit Servant.

Re-enter Fainall *and* Betty.

FAINALL.

Joy of your success, Mirabell; you look pleased.

133ff In so far as Mirabell's is a clear-headed infatuation, his love is founded on a rational acknowledgement and acceptance of the impetus of passions in human life. Such a recognition of the irrational is inseparable from the Augustan ideal of reasonableness as opposed to the dogmatic, *a priori*, system-building rationalism often identified with the previous century.

134 complaisance: obliging politeness (used ironically)

139 become her: suit her

143 sifted: examined carefully

MIRABELL.

Aye, I have been engaged in a matter of some sort of mirth, which is not yet ripe for discovery. I am glad this is not a cabal-night. I wonder, Fainall, that you who are married, and of consequence should be discreet, will suffer your wife to be of such a party.

FAINALL.

Faith, I am not jealous. Besides, most who are engaged are women and relations; and for the men, they are of a kind too contemptible to give scandal.

MIRABELL.

I am of another opinion. The greater the coxcomb, always the more scandal; for a woman who is not a fool can have but one reason for associating with a man that is.

FAINALL.

Are you jealous as often as you see Witwoud entertained by Millamant?

MIRABELL.

Of her understanding I am, if not of her person.

FAINALL.

You do her wrong; for, to give her her due, she has wit.

MIRABELL.

She has beauty enough to make any man think so, and complaisance enough not to contradict him who shall tell her so.

FAINALL.

For a passionate lover, me thinks you are a man somewhat too discerning in the failings of your mistress.

MIRABELL.

And for a discerning man, somewhat too passionate a lover; for I like her with all her faults; nay, like her for her faults. Her follies are so natural, or so artful, that they become her; and those affectations which in another woman would be odious, serve but to make her more agreeable. I'll tell thee Fainall, she once used me with that insolence, that in revenge I took her to pieces; sifted her and separated her failings; I studied'em,

144 by rote: by heart

146 used: habituated

150 frailties: weaknesses, shortcomings

152–54 Fainall's opinion, expressing neatly the opposition between love and marriage, the latter being commonly a financial arrangement, is partly challenged by the love and marriage of Mirabell and Millamant. For Fainall, a woman's charms, as distinct from her defects, are only a false veneer; for Mirabell, Millamant's defects are a part of her charm.

154 your own man: unattached, not in love

157 Squire: country gentleman, especially the chief landed proprietor in a district

and got'em by rote. The catalogue was so large that I was not without hopes one day or other to hate her heartily: to which end I so used myself to think of'em that at length, contrary to my design and expectation, they gave me every hour less and less disturbance; till in a few days it became habitual to me to remember 'em without being displeased. They are now grown as familiar to me as my own frailties; and in all probability, in a little time longer I shall like 'em as well.

FAINALL.
Marry her, marry her! Be half as well acquainted with her charms as you are with her defects, and my life on't, you are your own man again.

MIRABELL.
Say you so?

FAINALL.
Aye, aye, I have experience: I have a wife, and so forth.

Enter Messenger.

MESSENGER.
Is one Squire Witwoud here?

BETTY.
Yes; what's your business?

MESSENGER.
I have a letter for him, from his brother Sir Wilfull, which I am charged to deliver into his own hands.

BETTY.
He's in the next room, friend; that way. *Exit* Messenger.

MIRABELL.
What, is the chief of that noble family in town, Sir Wilfull Witwoud?

FAINALL.
He is expected today. Do you know him?

166–169 The relationships heighten the sense of a small, enclosed world.

171 travel: Travel was an essential part of the gentleman's education but it had already become a mere fashion instead of a humanist ideal.

171–74 Foolish English travellers on the Continent had already been satirized by Ben Jonson in *Volpone* in the figures of Sir and Lady Politick Would-Be. Such folly was often seen as the product of the aristocratic pretensions of the rising middle classes.

179 knight-errant: ironic reference to the medieval chivalric code

181 knight: pun on 'night'

181–82 a medlar … crab: a small brown fruit like an apple (eaten when decayed) grafted on a crab-apple (a sour wild apple). Witwoud, the urban fop ('all pulp') and his half-brother Sir Wilful, the country bumpkin (all core) are vividly contrasted.

MIRABELL.

I have seen him. He promises to be an extraordinary person; I think you have the honour to be related to him.

FAINALL.

Yes, he is half-brother to this Witwoud by a former wife, who was sister to my Lady Wishfort, my wife's mother. If you marry Millamant, you must call cousins too.

MIRABELL.

I had rather be his relation than his acquaintance.

FAINALL.

He comes to town in order to equip himself for travel.

MIRABELL.

For travel! Why the man I mean is above forty.

FAINALL.

No matter for that; 'tis for the honour of England that all Europe should know we have blockheads of all ages.

MIRABELL.

I wonder there is not an act of parliament to save the credit of the nation, and prohibit the exportation of fools.

FAINALL.

By no means; 'tis better as 'tis. 'Tis better to trade with a little loss, than to be quite eaten up with being over-stocked.

MIRABELL.

Pray, are the follies of this knight-errant and those of the squire his brother anything related?

FAINALL.

Not at all; Witwoud grows by the knight, like a medlar grafted on crab. One will melt in your mouth, and t'other set your teeth on edge; one is all pulp, and the other all core.

MIRABELL.

So one will be rotten before he be ripe, and the other will be rotten without ever being ripe at all.

186ff Sir Wilfull (see above) offers a country alternative to the urban milieu, a somewhat stereotypical, though not unreal, rustic simplicity against the artificial decorums of upper-class life in London.

187–88 An allusion to Caliban in Shakespeare's *The Tempest* adapted by Dryden and D'Avenant.

191 commonplace: a commonplace book for recording memorable remarks or passages; popular since the Elizabethan age

194 exceptious: inclined to raise objections

196 raillery: good-humoured ridicule, an essential feature of Restoration wit construe an affront: interpret an insult

200 Our first encounter of Witwoud's pompous style

202 Ironic response from Mirabell.

FAINALL.

Sir Wilfull is an odd mixture of bashfulness and obstinacy. But when he's drunk, he's as loving as the monster in *The Tempest,* and much after the same manner. To give t'other his due, he has something of good nature and does not always want wit.

MIRABELL.

Not always; but as often as his memory fails him, and his commonplace of comparisons. He is a fool with a good memory and some few scraps of other folks' wit. He is one whose conversation can never be approved, yet it is now and then to be endured. He has indeed one good quality, he is not exceptious; for he so passionately affects the reputation of understanding raillery, that he will construe an affront into a jest, and call downright rudeness and ill language satire and fire.

FAINALL.

If you have a mind to finish his picture, you have an opportunity to do it at full length. Behold the original!

Enter Witwoud.

WITWOUD.

Afford me your compassion, my dears! Pity me, Fainall! Mirabell, pity me!

MIRABELL.

I do from my soul.

FAINALL.

Why, what's the matter?

WITWOUD.

No letters for me, Betty?

BETTY.

Did not the messenger bring you one but now, sir?

WITWOUD.

Aye, but no other?

BETTY.

No, sir.

210–13 The string of hackneyed analogies suggests an interesting link between social and literary ritual.
a panegyric … sermon: formal speech in high praise of the dead as part of a religious discourse at the funeral.

211 commendatory verses: formal verses in high praise of another poet.

212–13 epistle dedicatory: formal note of dedication to a patron preceding the actual contents of a book

217 half a fool: If Sir Wilfull is only half a fool because he is half-brother to Witwoud, then the latter by implication is a full-blown fool.

218 *le drôle*: French for 'an amusing fellow' ('droll' in English)

219ff By inquiring about Fainall's wife and domestic life, Witwoud breaks a typically modish and trivial rule of social decorum.

WITWOUD.

That's hard, that's very hard. A messenger, a mule, a beast of burden! He has brought me a letter from the fool my brother, as heavy as a panegyric in a funeral sermon, or a copy of commendatory verses from one poet to another. And what's worse, 'tis as sure a forerunner of the author as an epistle dedicatory.

MIRABELL.

A fool, and your brother Witwoud!

WITWOUD.

Aye, aye, my half-brother. My half-brother he is, no nearer upon honour.

MIRABELL.

Then 'tis possible he may be but half a fool.

WITWOUD.

Good, good, Mirabell , *le drôle!* Good, good; hang him, don't let's talk of him. Fainall, how does your lady? Gad, I say anything in the world to get this fellow out of my head. I beg pardon that I should ask a man of pleasure, and the town, a question at once so foreign and domestic. But I talk like an old maid at a marriage, I don't know what I say; but she's the best woman in the world.

FAINALL.

'Tis well you don't know what you say, or else your commendation would go near to make me either vain or jealous.

WITWOUD.

No man in town lives well with a wife but Fainall. Your judgment, Mirabell.

MIRABELL.

You had better step and ask his wife, if you would be credibly informed.

WITWOUD.

Mirabell.

238 spleen: depression believed to be caused by disease of the spleen; a fashionable malady associated with wealth and indolence.

244 repartee: witty reply

248ff Under the guise of friendly support, Witwoud ridicules Petulant. The friendship of the fools is no more than a travesty and thereby highlights the animosities underlying polite relationships.

250 smattering: slight, superficial knowledge

MIRABELL.

Aye.

WITWOUD.

My dear, I ask ten thousand pardons. Gad, I have forgot what I was going to say to you!

MIRABELL.

I thank you heartily, heartily.

WITWOUD.

No, but prithee excuse me: my memory is such a memory.

MIRABELL.

Have a care of such apologies, Witwoud; for I never knew a fool but he affected to complain, either of the spleen or his memory.

FAINALL.

What have you done with Petulant?

WITWOUD.

He's reckoning his money, my money it was. I have no luck today.

FAINALL.

You may allow him to win of you at play, for you are sure to be too hard for him at repartee; since you monopolise the wit that is between you; the fortune must be his of course.

MIRABELL.

I don't find that Petulant confesses the superiority of wit to be your talent, Witwoud.

WITWOUD.

Come, come, you are malicious now, and would breed debates. Petulant's my friend, and a very honest fellow, and a very pretty fellow, and has a smattering—faith and troth, a pretty deal of an odd sort of a small wit: nay, I'll do him justice. I'm his friend, I won't wrong him neither. And if he had but any judgment in the world, he would not be altogether contemptible. Come, come, don't detract from the merits of my friend.

255 over-nicely: in a very refined manner

257 bum-baily: bum-bailiff who would arrest debtors by touching them on the back

275–76 Witwoud gives a standard view of the 'philosophy' of the Restoration wit or rake.

277 positive: dogmatic, cocksure

FAINALL.
You don't take your friend to be over-nicely bred?

WITWOUD.
No, no, hang him, the rogue has no manners at all, that I must own. No more breeding than a bum-baily, that I grant you. 'Tis pity, faith; the fellow has fire and life.

MIRABELL.
What, courage?

WITWOUD.
Hum, faith, I don't know as to that, I can't say as to that. Yes, faith, in a controversy he'll contradict anybody.

MIRABELL.
Though 'twere a man whom he feared, or a woman whom he loved.

WITWOUD.
Well, well, he does not always think before he speaks; we have all our failings. You're too hard upon him, you are, faith. Let me excuse him. I can defend most of his faults, except one or two. One he has, that's the truth on't; if he were my brother, I could not acquit him. That, indeed, I could wish were otherwise.

MIRABELL.
Aye, marry, what's that Witwoud?

WITWOUD.
Oh, pardon me! Expose the infirmities of my friend! No, my dear, excuse me there.

FAINALL.
What, I warrant he's unsincere, or 'tis some such trifle.

WITWOUD.
No, no, what if he be? 'Tis no matter for that, his wit will excuse that. A wit should no more be sincere than a woman constant; one argues a decay of parts, as t'other of beauty.

MIRABELL.
Maybe you think him too positive?

282 **natural parts**: This refers to a nature that has not been moulded or developed by murture. A 'natural' also meant a fool or idiot.

290 **unseasonable**: not appropriate to the occasion

WITWOUD.

No, no his being positive is an incentive to argument, and keeps up conversation.

FAINALL.

Too illiterate?

WITWOUD.

That! that's his happiness; his want of learning gives him the more opportunities to show his natural parts.

MIRABELL.

He wants words?

WITWOUD.

Aye, but I like him for that now; for his want of words gives me the pleasure very often to explain his meaning.

FAINALL.

He's impudent?

WITWOUD.

No, that's not it.

MIRABELL.

Vain?

WITWOUD.

No.

MIRABELL.

What! he speaks unseasonable truths sometimes, because he has not wit enough to invent an evasion?

WITWOUD.

Truths! ha! ha! ha! No, no, since you will have it, I mean he never speaks truth at all, that's all. He will lie like a chambermaid, or a woman of quality's porter. Now that is a fault.

Enter Coachman.

COACHMAN.

Is Master Petulant here, mistress?

BETTY.

Yes.

297 One of Petulant's ploys to give himself importance.

301 cinnamon-water: sugar, spirits and cinnamon mixed in hot water—considered good for digestion (for 'a bawd troubled with wind')

302ff By making Petulant proceed to absurd lengths in his attempts to inflate his status – calling for himself – Congreve plays on the problem of dissembling and identity.

302 strumpets: prostitutes; a woman who runs a brothel

302–03 bawd … wind: suffering from flatulence

toasting: drinking to the health or in honour of someone

307 trulls: prostitutes

318 hackney-coach: horse-carriage for hire

COACHMAN.
Three gentlewomen in the coach would speak with him.

FAINALL.
Oh brave Petulant! Three!

BETTY.
I'll tell him.

COACHMAN.
You must bring two dishes of chocolate and a glass of cinnamon-water. *Exeunt* Betty *and* Coachman.

WITWOUD.
That should be for two fasting strumpets, and a bawd troubled with wind. Now you may know what the three are.

MIRABELL.
You are very free with your friend's acquaintance.

WITWOUD.
Aye, aye, friendship without freedom is as dull as love without enjoyment, or wine without toasting; but to tell you a secret, these are trulls that he allows coach-hire, and something more, by the week, to call on him once a day at public places.

MIRABELL.
How!

WITWOUD.
You shall see he won't go to 'em because there's no more company here to take notice of him. Why, this is nothing to what he used to do; before he found out this way, I have known him call for himself.

FAINALL.
Call for himself? What dost thou mean?

WITWOUD.
Mean! Why, he would slip you out of this chocolate-house, just when you had been talking to him. As soon as your back was turned, whip, he was gone! Then trip to his lodging, clap on a hood and scarf, and mask, slap into a hackney-coach, and drive hither to the door again in a trice, where he would

325 stays: waits for you.
326 'Sbud: the oath *God's blood*
327 midwife: woman assisting at childbirth
whoremaster: brothel-keeper
328 Pox on 'em: a curse (pox = syphilis)
329 snivel: weep (with running nose)
333 condition: high rank, status
337 rub off: push off
340 queens: pun on 'quean' (prostitute)
341 Roxolanas: Roxolana is the Sultana in D'Avenant's *The Siege of Rhodes.* In the seventeenth century, Roxolana also referred to a favourite mistress.

send in for himself; that I mean, call for himself, wait for himself; nay, and what's more, not finding himself, sometimes leave a letter for himself.

MIRABELL.

I confess this is something extraordinary. I believe he waits for himself now, he is so long a-coming. Oh! I ask his pardon.

Enter Petulant *and* Betty.

BETTY.

Sir, the coach stays.

PETULANT.

Well, well; I come. 'Sbud, a man had as good be a professed midwife as a professed whoremaster, at this rate! To be knocked up and raised at all hours, and in all places! Pox on 'em, I won't come! D'ye hear, tell 'em I won't come. Let 'em snivel and cry their hearts out.

FAINAL.

You are very cruel, Petulant.

PETULANT.

All's one, let it pass. I have a humour to be cruel.

MIRABELL.

I hope they are not persons of condition that you use at this rate.

PETULANT.

Condition! Condition's a dried fig, if I am not in humour! By this hand, if they were your—a—a—your what-d'ye-call-'ems themselves, they must wait or rub off, if I want appetite.

MIRABELL

What–d'ye-call-'ems! What are they, Witwoud?

WITWOUD.

Empresses, my dear; by your what-d'ye-call-'ems he means sultana queens.

PETULANT.

Aye, Roxolanas.

346 Harkee: 'hark ye'
347 caterwauling: quarrelling as of cats
348 conventicle: clandestine meeting of nonconformists, religious dissenters often marked by chanting. These meetings were no longer banned.
356 trundle: roll along, 'make off'
paint: make-up
357 continence: sexual restraint
dissembled: put on
361 pretensions: claims

MIRABELL.

Cry you mercy.

FAINALL.

Witwoud says they are—

PETULANT.

What does he say th'are?

WITWOUD.

I? Fine ladies, I say.

PETULANT.

Pass on, Witwoud. Harkee, by this light his relations: two co heiresses his cousins, and an old aunt, that loves caterwauling better than a conventicle.

WITWOUD.

Ha! ha! ha! I had a mind to see how the rogue would come off. Ha! ha! ha! Gad, I can't be angry with him, if he had said they were my mother and my sisters.

MIRABELL.

No!

WITWOUD.

No; the rogue's wit and readiness of invention charm me. Dear Petulant!

BETTY.

They are gone, sir, in great anger.

PETULANT.

Enough, let 'em trundle. Anger helps complexion, saves paint.

FAINALL.

This continence is all dissembled; this is in order to have something to brag of the next time he makes court to Millamant, and swear he has abandoned the whole sex for her sake.

MIRABELL.

Have you not left off your impudent pretensions there yet? I shall cut your throat some time or other, Petulant, about that business.

370 interpreter: Witwoud (presumably)
381–82 Snug's the word: Petulant refuses to divulge the secret.
383 raillery: teasing

PETULANT.
Aye, aye, let that pass. There are other throats to be cut.

MIRABELL.
Meaning mine, sir?

PETULANT.
Not I. I mean nobody; I know nothing. But there are uncles and nephews in the world, and they may be rivals. What then? All's one for that.

MIRABELL.
How! Harkee Petulant, come hither. Explain, or I shall call your interpreter.

PETULANT.
Explain! I know nothing. Why, you have an uncle, have you not, lately come to town, and lodges by my Lady Wishfort's?

MIRABELL.
True.

PETULANT.
Why, that's enough. You and he are not friends; and if he should marry and have a child, you may be disinherited, ha?

MIRABELL.
Where hast thou stumbled upon all this truth?

PETULANT.
All's one for that; why, then say I know something.

MIRABELL.
Come, thou art an honest fellow, Petulant, and make love to my mistress, thou sha't, faith. What hast thou heard of my uncle?

PETULANT.
I? Nothing. If throats are to be cut, let swords clash! Snug's the word; I shrug and am silent.

MIRABELL.
Oh, raillery, raillery! Come, I know thou art in the women's secrets. What, you're a cabalist; I know you stayed at

388–89 dead whiting's eye: the whiting is a white fish; its dead eye would be dull and glazed.

389 pearl of Orient: The East was famous for brilliant and precious pearls.

390 by thee: beside you

Mercury is by the sun: Mercury, being the nearest planet to the sun, is invisible in the sun's dazzling light.

403 uncertain: unpredictable and whimsical

Millamant's last night, after I went. Was there any mention made of my uncle or me? Tell me. If thou hadst but good nature equal to thy wit, Petulant, Tony Witwoud, who is now thy competitor in fame, would show as dim by thee as a dead whiting's eye by a pearl of Orient; he would no more be seen by thee than Mercury is by the sun. Come, I'm sure thou wo't tell me.

PETULANT.
If I do, will you grant me common sense then for the future?

MIRABELL.
Faith, I'll do what I can for thee; and I'll pray that Heaven may grant it thee in the meantime.

PETULANT.
Well, harkee.

Mirabell *and* Petulant *talk apart.*

FAINALL.
Petulant and you both will find Mirabell as warm a rival as a lover.

WITWOUD.
Pshaw! pshaw! That she laughs Petulant is plain. And for my part, but that it is almost a fashion to admire her, I should—harkee, to tell you a secret, but let it go no further; between friends, I shall never break my heart for her.

FAINALL.
How!

WITWOUD.
She's handsome; but she's a sort of an uncertain woman.

FAINALL.
I thought you had died for her.

WITWOUD.
Umh—no—

FAINALL.
She has wit.

407 demme: damn me

408 Cleopatra: Egyptian queen at the time of Julius Caesar, Antony and Octavius, renowned for her beauty.

415 Quaker: a religious sect (Society of Friends) founded by George Fox (1648–50) and devoted to peace, simplicity of dress and speech and priestless religious meetings. The Quaker would hate a parrot because of its talkativeness.

416 fishmonger … frost: because the frost makes fishing difficult

420 fobbed: cheated

421 hearken: listen

423 humourist: whimsical person

424ff Mirabell and Petulant, who had been talking apart, presumably come to the centre or the foreground.

425 quintessence: most essential part

428 *tête à tête*: together in private, face to face

WITWOUD.

'Tis what she will hardly allow anybody else. Now, demme, I should hate that, if she were as handsome as Cleopatra. Mirabell is not so sure of her as he thinks for.

FAINALL.

Why do you think so?

WITWOUD.

We stayed pretty late there last night, and heard something of an uncle to Mirabell, who is lately come to town, and is between him and the best part of his estate. Mirabell and he are at some distance, as my Lady Wishfort has been told; and you know she hates Mirabell worse than a Quaker hates a parrot, or than a fishmonger hates a hard frost. Whether this uncle has seen Mrs. Millamant or not, I cannot say; but there were items of such a treaty being in embryo, and if it should come to life, poor Mirabell would be in some sort unfortunately fobbed, i'faith.

FAINALL.

'Tis impossible Millamant should hearken to it.

WITWOUD.

Faith, my dear, I can't tell; she's a woman and a kind of a humourist.

MIRABELL.

And is this the sum of what you could collect last night?

PETULANT.

The quintessence. May be Witwoud knows more; he stayed longer. Besides, they never mind him; they say anything before him.

MIRABELL.

I thought you had been the greatest favourite.

PETULANT.

Aye, *tête à tête,* but not in public, because I make remarks.

MIRABELL.

You do?

436 the Mall: a gravel walk bordered by trees in St. James's Park, originally the alley in which the game of mall was played, later a fashionable promenade. It is now known as Pall Mall.

437 walk in the park: a common social pastime of the upper classes enabling them to see and meet each other

445 quick: alive, lively

446 severe: satirical of other walkers

448ff Mirabell's criticism of the 'senseless ribaldry' of the fools seems to expose the spuriousness of polite culture.

448 accessory to: contribute to

putting … countenance: embarrassing them

450 ribaldry: indecent language

PETULANT.

Aye, aye, pox, I'm malicious, man! Now he's soft, you know, they are not in awe of him. The fellow's well-bred, he's what you call a—what-d'ye-call-'em, a fine gentleman, but he's silly withal.

MIRABELL.

I thank you. I know as much as my curiosity requires. Fainall, are you for the Mall?

FAINALL.

Aye, I'll take a turn before dinner.

WITWOUD.

Aye, we'll all walk in the park; the ladies talked of being there.

MIRABELL.

I thought you were obliged to watch for your brother Sir Wilfull's arrival.

WITWOUD.

No, no, he comes to his aunt's, my Lady Wishfort. Pox on him! I shall be troubled with him too; what shall I do with the fool?

PETULANT.

Beg him for his estate, that I may beg you afterwards; and so have but one trouble with you both.

WITWOUD.

Oh, rare Petulant! Thou art as quick as a fire in a frosty morning; thou shalt to the Mall with us, and we'll be very severe.

PETULANT.

Enough, I'm in a humour to be severe.

MIRABELL.

Are you? Pray then walk by yourselves. Let not us be accessory to your putting the ladies out of countenance with your senseless ribaldry, which you roar out aloud as often as they pass by you; and when you have made a handsome woman blush, then you think you have been severe.

458 out of countenance: Mirabell's rebuke clearly exposes the false wit of *parvemus* aping gentlemanly manners without gentlemanly breeding. This kind of bad manners is to be contrasted with the somewhat rustic manners of Sir Wilful.

PETULANT.

What, what? Then let 'em show their innocence by not understanding what they hear, or else show their discretion by not hearing what they would not be thought to understand.

MIRABELL.

But hast not thou then sense enough to know that thou ought'st to be most ashamed thyself, when thou hast put another out of countenance?

PETULANT.

No I, by this hand! I always take blushing either for a sign of guilt or ill-breeding.

MIRABELL.

I confess you ought to think so. You are in the right, that you may plead the error of your judgment in defence of your practice.

Where modesty's ill manners, 'tis but fit
That impudence and malice pass for wit.

Exeunt.

[II] St. James's Park: If the Chocolate House is frequented by men, St. James's Park, near the Buckingham Palace, is the fashionable meeting-place for men and women. References in the previous Act to the Mall, a walk in the park and Rosamund's Pond prepare us for the shift in locale in this Act.

In this scene, the feline animosity lurking underneath the relationship between Mrs. Fainall and Mrs. Marwood offers a parallel to the Fainall-Mirabell relationship in the previous act. The repetition suggests that falseness, malice and distrust are integral to the world of the play. Similarly, male obsession with and definition of women in Act I is balanced by the female point of view on men. The swiftness with which the jealous lover turns into the disgusted ex-lover highlights the absence of love in a society restless in its pursuit of sexual pleasure and money. The hatred that the women profess for men is of course false and hypocritical, but perhaps there is in it an element of bitterness stemming from their helpless dependence on men.

3 doting or averse: too fond or too hateful

12 sweets of life: pleasures of life

17 in compliance with: in line with

18 free: frank

19 of force: of necessity

23–24 or soon or late: sooner or later

25–26 profess a libertine: declare yourself as a libertine, that is unrestrained in amours. Originally, a libertine was one who had a free-thinking, antinomian attitude towards religion, morality and related values

Act II, Scene I

St. James's Park.
Enter Mrs. Fainall *and* Mrs. Marwood.

MRS. FAINALL.

Aye, aye, dear Marwood, if we will be happy, we must find the means in ourselves, and among ourselves. Men are ever in extremes, either doting or averse. While they are lovers, if they have fire and sense, their jealousies are insupportable. And when they cease to love (we ought to think at least) they loathe; they look upon us with horror and distaste; they meet us like the ghosts of what we were, and as such fly from us.

MRS. MARWOOD.

True, 'tis an unhappy circumstance of life, that love should ever die before us; and that the man so often should outlive the lover. But say what you will, 'tis better to be left than never to have been loved. To pass our youth in dull indifference, to refuse the sweets of life because they once must leave us, is as preposterous as to wish to have been born old, because we one day must be old. For my part, my youth may wear and waste, but it shall never rust in my possession.

MRS. FAINALL.

Then it seems you dissemble an aversion to mankind, only in compliance with my mother's humour.

MRS. MARWOOD.

Certainly. To be free, I have no taste of those insipid dry discourses with which our sex of force must entertain themselves, apart from men. We may affect endearments to each other, profess eternal friendships, and seem to dote like lovers; but 'tis not in our natures long to persevere. Love will resume his empire in our breasts; and every heart, or soon or late, receive and readmit him as its lawful tyrant.

MRS. FAINALL.

Bless me, how have I been deceived! Why you profess a libertine!

31 **inveterately: suggesting a deep-rooted hatred**

33 **transcendently: surpassingly**

meritoriously: i.e., meriting or deserving hatred

40 **an Amazon, a Penthesilea: famous Queen of the Amazons, a fabulous race of female warriors**

MRS. MARWOOD.

You see my friendship by my freedom. Come, be as sincere, acknowledge that your sentiments agree with mine.

MRS. FAINALL.

Never!

MRS. MARWOOD.

You hate mankind?

MRS. FAINALL.

Heartily, inveterately.

MRS. MARWOOD.

Your husband?

MRS. FAINALL.

Most transcendently; aye, though I say it, meritoriously.

MRS. MARWOOD.

Give me your hand upon it.

MRS. FAINALL.

There.

MRS. MARWOOD.

I join with you; what I have said has been to try you.

MRS. FAINALL.

Is it possible? Dost thou hate those vipers, men?

MRS. MARWOOD.

I have done hating 'em, and am now come to despise 'em; the next thing I have to do, is eternally to forget 'em.

MRS. FAINALL.

There spoke the spirit of an Amazon, a Penthesilea.

MRS. MARWOOD.

And yet I am thinking sometimes to carry my aversion further.

MRS. FAINALL.

How?

MRS. MARWOOD.

Faith, by marrying; if I could but find one that loved me very

44 sensible: sensitive, conscious
46 cuckold: a man whose wife is sexually unfaithful
51 rack: instrument of torture
54 change colour: blush. Mrs. Marwood betrays her passion for Mirabell

well and would be thoroughly sensible of ill usage, I think I should do myself the violence of undergoing the ceremony.

MRS. FAINALL.
You would not make him cuckold?

MRS. MARWOOD.
No, but I'd make him believe I did, and that's as bad.

MRS. FAINALL.
Why had not you as good do it?

MRS. MARWOOD.
Oh, if he should ever discover it, he would then know the worst, and be out of his pain; but I would have him ever to continue upon the rack of fear and jealousy.

MRS. FAINALL.
Ingenious mischief! Would thou wert married to Mirabell.

MRS. MARWOOD.
Would I were!

MRS. FAINALL.
You change colour.

MRS. MARWOOD.
Because I hate him.

MRS. FAINALL.
So do I; but I can hear him named. But what reason have you to hate him in particular?

MRS. MARWOOD.
I never loved him; he is, and always was, insufferably proud.

MRS. FAINALL.
By the reason you give for your aversion, one would think it dissembled; for you have laid a fault to his charge of which his enemies must acquit him.

MRS. MARWOOD.
Oh, then it seems you are one of his favorable enemies! Methinks you look a little pale, and now you flush again.

66	turned short upon me: turned back quickly before the expected time
66–67	husband as spy
68	opportunely: in a well-timed moment
70ff	Fainall and Mrs. Fainall address each other with patently false, exaggerated endearments
80	relation: story
81	fain: gladly

MRS. FAINALL.
Do I? I think I am a little sick o' the sudden.

MRS. MARWOOD.
What ails you?

MRS. FAINALL.
My husband. Don't you see him? He turned short upon me unawares, and has almost overcome me.

Enter Fainall *and* Mirabell.

MRS. MARWOOD.
Ha! ha! ha! He comes opportunely for you.

MRS. FAINALL.
For you, for he has brought Mirabell with him.

FAINALL.
My dear.

MRS. FAINALL.
My soul!

FAINALL.
You don't look well today, child.

MRS. FAINALL.
D'ye think so?

MIRABELL.
He is the only man that does, madam.

MRS. FAINALL.
The only man that would tell me so at least; and the only man from whom I could hear it without mortification.

FAINALL.
Oh my dear, I am satisfied of your tenderness; I know you cannot resent anything from me, especially what is an effect of my concern.

MRS. FAINALL.
Mr. Mirabell, my mother interrupted you in a pleasant relation last night; I would fain hear it out.

84 a humour more prevailing: an inclination stronger than

85–88 In this fashionable world, husband and wife walking together could cause a scandal.

92ff Fainall's fear of success or accomplishment suggests in its constant need for stimulation and excitement an appetite cloyed by pleasure.

95 Alexander: Alexander the Great

MIRABELL.

The persons concerned in that affair have yet a tolerable reputation. I am afraid Mr. Fainall will be censorious.

MRS. FAINALL.

He has a humour more prevailing than his curiosity, and will willingly dispense with the hearing of one scandalous story, to avoid giving an occasion to make another by being seen to walk with his wife. This way, Mr. Mirabell, and I dare promise you will oblige us both.

Exeunt Mrs. Fainall *and* Mirabell.

FAINALL.

Excellent creature ! Well, sure if I should live to be rid of my wife, I should be a miserable man.

MRS. MARWOOD.

Aye !

FAINALL.

For having only that one hope, the accomplishment of it, of consequence must put an end to all my hopes; and what a wretch is he who must survive his hopes! Nothing remains when that day comes, but to sit down and weep like Alexander, when he wanted other worlds to conquer.

MRS. MARWOOD.

Will you not follow 'em?

FAINALL.

Faith, I think not.

MRS. MARWOOD.

Pray let us; I have a reason.

FAINALL.

You are not jealous?

MRS. MARWOOD.

Of whom?

FAINALL.

Of Mirabell.

105	intimate: suggest
109	insensible: insensitive
118	struck fire: as from two flint-stones
121ff	Marriage becomes a convenient cover for promiscuity
121	oversee: ignore

MRS. MARWOOD.

If I am, is it inconsistent with my love to you that I am tender of your honour?

FAINALL.

You would intimate then, as if there were a fellow-feeling between my wife and him.

MRS. MARWOOD.

I think she does not hate him to that degree she would be thought.

FAINALL.

But he, I fear, is too insensible.

MRS. MARWOOD.

It may be you are deceived.

FAINALL.

It may be so. I do now begin to apprehend it.

MRS. MARWOOD.

What?

FAINALL.

That I have been deceived, madam, and you are false.

MRS. MARWOOD.

That I am false! What mean you?

FAINALL.

To let you know I see through all your little arts. Come, you both love him; and both have equally dissembled your aversion. Your mutual jealousies of one another have made you clash till you have both struck fire. I have seen the warm confession reddening on your cheeks, and sparkling from your eyes.

MRS. MARWOOD.

You do me wrong.

FAINALL.

I do not. 'Twas for my ease to oversee and wilfully neglect the gross advances made him by my wife; that by permitting her to be engaged, I might continue unsuspected in my pleasures,

125 nodding: sleeping
127 wherewithal: with what
131ff Fainall's clinical exposure of Mrs. Marwood's thwarted and warped passion for Mirabell makes her vulnerability more acceptable than his cold-blooded villainy. As we see in this scene, even Mrs. Marwood (like most of the women in the play) is a victim of male manipulation
133 interposing: interfering
134 to make discoveries of: to expose
135 officious: over-eager
141 pious: devoted (ironic)
147 upbraid: reproach
148 inviolate: not violated or corrupted

and take you oftener to my arms in full security. But could you think, because the nodding husband would not wake, that e'er the watchful lover slept?

MRS. MARWOOD.

And wherewithal can you reproach me?

FAINALL.

With infidelity, with loving of another, with love of Mirabell.

MRS. MARWOOD.

'Tis false. I challenge you to show an instance that can confirm your groundless accusation. I hate him.

FAINALL.

And wherefore do you hate him? He is insensible and your resentment follows his neglect. An instance? The injuries you have done him are a proof, your interposing in his love. What cause had you to make discoveries of his pretended passion? To undeceive the credulous aunt, and be the officious obstacle of his match with Millamant?

MRS. MARWOOD.

My obligations to my lady urged me; I had professed a friendship to her, and could not see her easy nature so abused by that dissembler.

FAINALL.

What, was it conscience then? Professed a friendship ! Oh, the pious friendships of the female sex !

MRS. MARWOOD.

More tender, more sincere, and more enduring, than all the vain and empty vows of men, whether professing love to us or mutual faith to one another.

FAINALL.

Ha! ha! ha! you are my wife's friend too.

MRS. MARWOOD.

Shame and ingratitude ! Do you reproach me? You, you upbraid me ! Have I been false to her through strict fidelity to you, and sacrificed my friendship to keep my love inviolate?

153	reproof: rebuke, reproach
162	prevent: forestall
170	indigent: poor, needy
172	prodigality: excess, lavishness
173	ere: before
173ff	Mrs. Marwood's jealousy has prompted her to obstruct the marriage of Mirabell and Millamant but Fainall is untouched by even such distorted emotional spontaneity, guided as he is entirely by financial calculations. To put things in their right perspective, we must remind ourselves, however, that nearly every one in the play is running after money and legacy.

And have you the baseness to charge me with the guilt, ummindful of the merit! To you it should be meritorious, that I have been vicious; and do you reflect that guilt upon me, which should lie buried in your bosom?

FAINALL.

You misinterpret my reproof. I meant but to remind you of the slight account you once could make of strictest ties, when set in comparison with your love to me.

MRS. MARWOOD.

'Tis false; you urged it with deliberate malice! 'Twas spoke in scorn, and I never will forgive it.

FAINALL.

Your guilt, not your resentment, begets your rage. If yet you loved, you could forgive a jealousy; but you are stung to find you are discovered.

MRS. MARWOOD.

It shall be all discovered. You too shall be discovered; be sure you shall. I can but be exposed. If I do it myself, I shall prevent your baseness.

FAINALL.

Why, what will you do?

MRS. MARWOOD.

Disclose it to your wife; own what has passed between us.

FAINALL.

Frenzy!

MRS. MARWOOD.

By all my wrongs I'll do't! I'll publish to the world the injuries you have done me, both in my fame and fortune! With both I trusted you, you bankrupt in honour, as indigent of wealth.

FAINALL.

Your fame I have preserved. Your fortune has been bestowed as the prodigality of your love would have it, in pleasures which we both have shared. Yet had not you been false, I had ere this

175 incensed: very angry
176–77 forfeited … fortune: lost the right to half of her fortune
179 squander: spend wastefully, lavishly
182 imprisoned, fettered: definition of marriage exemplifying Restoration wit
184 of proof: of proven strength
185 wedlock: marriage
190ff Are we to see in this (and the preceding section) an emotional outburst threatening the deceiving and self-deceiving gaiety of Restoration society? In any case, emotions are strangely located in this world, hidden behind a mask to ensure the success of intrigue.
190 loathe: dislike intensely
usage: treatment
191 asperse: slander, accuse

repaid it. 'Tis true, had you permitted Mirabell with Millamant to have stolen their marriage, my lady had been incensed beyond all means of reconcilement; Millamant had forfeited the moiety of her fortune, which then would have descended to my wife. And wherefore did I marry, but to make lawful prize of a rich widow's wealth, and squander it on love and you?

MRS. MARWOOD.

Deceit and frivolous pretence !

FAINALL.

Death, am I not married? What's pretence? Am I not imprisoned, fettered? Have I not a wife? Nay a wife that was a widow, a young widow, a handsome widow; and would be again a widow, but that I have a heart of proof, and something of a constitution to bustle through the ways of wedlock and this world. Will you yet be reconciled to truth and me?

MRS. MARWOOD.

Impossible. Truth and you are inconsistent. I hate you, and shall forever.

FAINALL.

For loving you?

MRS. MARWOOD.

I loathe the name of love after such usage; and next to the guilt with which you would asperse me, I scorn you most. Farewell !

FAINALL.

Nay, we must not part thus.

MRS. MARWOOD.

Let me go.

FAINALL.

Come, I'm sorry.

MRS. MARWOOD.

I care not, let me go. Break my hands, do! I'd leave 'em to get loose.

207 loathe, detest, abhor: a string of synonyms for rhetorical emphasis
209 extravagance: unreasonable excess
211 forbear: be patient
215 'Sdeath: *God's death*
216 mask: worn for disguise, the mask was often used in secret or illicit amours and assignations

FAINALL.

I would not hurt you for the world. Have I no other hold to keep you here?

MRS. MARWOOD.

Well, I have deserved it all.

FAINALL.

You know I love you.

MRS. MARWOOD.

Poor dissembling! Oh, that—Well, it is not yet—

FAINALL.

What? what is it not? What is it not yet? It is not yet too late—

MRS. MARWOOD.

No, it is not yet too late; I have that comfort.

FAINALL.

It is, to love another.

MRS. MARWOOD.

But not to loathe, detest, abhor mankind, myself, and the whole treacherous world.

FAINALL.

Nay, this is extravagance. Come, I ask your pardon. No tears. I was to blame; I could not love you and be easy in my doubts. Pray, forbear. I believe you. I'm convinced I've done you wrong; and anyway, every way will make amends. I'll hate my wife yet more, damn her ! I'll part with her, rob her of all she's worth, and we'll retire somewhere, anywhere, to another world. I'll marry thee; be pacified. 'Sdeath, they come; hide your face, your tears. You have a mask; wear it a moment. This way, this way. Be persuaded. *Exeunt.*

Enter Mirabell *and* Mrs. Fainall.

MRS. FAINALL.

They are here yet.

221 offensive: revolting

224ff There is an uneasiness built into Mirabell's treatment of Mrs. Fainall inseparable from his calculating rationalism throughout the play.

230 idol: a false god, a lifeless copy. Reputation may be a mere idol, but it demands and extracts worship.
familiarities: intimacies

231 that consequence: Mrs. Fainall's pregnancy

233–34 lavish of his morals: of loose morals

234 interested and professing: affecting friendship in order to further a self-interest

238 addresses: courtship

242 privy to: secretly aware of

MIRABELL.

They are turning into the other walk.

MRS. FAINALL.

While I only hated my husband, I could bear to see him; but since I have despised him, he's too offensive.

MIRABELL.

Oh, you should hate with prudence.

MRS. FAINALL.

Yes, for I have loved with indiscretion.

MIRABELL.

You should have just so much disgust for your husband as may be sufficient to make you relish your lover.

MRS. FAINALL.

You have been the cause that I have loved without bounds, and would you set limits to that aversion of which you have been the occasion? Why did you make me marry this man?

MIRABELL.

Why do we daily commit disagreeable and dangerous actions? To save that idol, reputation. If the familiarities of our loves had produced that consequence of which you were apprehensive, where could you have fixed a father's name with credit, but on a husband? I knew Fainall to be a man lavish of his morals, an interested and professing friend, a false and a designing lover; yet one whose wit and outward fair behaviour have gained a reputation with the town enough to make that woman stand excused who has suffered herself to be won by his addresses. A better man ought not to have been sacrificed to the occasion; a worse had not answered to the purpose. When you are weary of him, you know your remedy.

MRS. FAINALL.

I ought to stand in some degree of credit with you, Mirabell.

MIRABELL.

In justice to you, I have made you privy to my whole design, and put it in your power to ruin or advance my fortune.

254 like Mosca ... terms: In Ben Jonson's *Volpone* (1606), Mosca, the parasite-servant refuses to deliver Volpone from judgment even when the latter offers him half the spoils. Mosca wants all, and the result is that both he and Volpone are ruined.

257 imposture: fraudulent deception

betimes: in good time

264 carry it: conduct it

MRS. FAINALL.

Whom have you instructed to represent your pretended uncle?

MIRABELL.

Waitwell, my servant.

MRS. FAINALL.

He is an humble servant to Foible, my mother's woman, and may win her to your interest.

MIRABELL.

Care is taken for that. She is won and worn by this time. They were married this morning.

MRS. FAINALL.

Who?

MIRABELL.

Waitwell and Foible. I would not tempt my servant to betray me by trusting him too far. If your mother, in hopes to ruin me, should consent to marry my pretended uncle, he might, like Mosca in *The Fox,* stand upon terms; so I made him sure beforehand.

MRS. FAINALL.

So, if my poor mother is caught in a contract, you will discover the imposture betimes, and release her by producing a certificate of her gallant's former marriage.

MIRABELL.

Yes, upon condition she consent to my marriage with her niece, and surrender the moiety of her fortune in her possession.

MRS. FAINALL.

She talked last night of endeavouring at a match between Millamant and your uncle.

MIRABELL.

That was by Foible's direction, and my instruction, that she might seem to carry it more privately.

MRS. FAINALL.

Well, I have an opinion of your success, for I believe my lady will do anything to get a husband; and when she has this,

270–71 what a butler ... napkin: butlers often presented dinner napkins in the form of interesting figures

272ff Geriatric lust is a common theme in Congreve, if not in all Restoration Comedy. In the claustrophobic and unreal world of coquetry, old age is a terrifying prospect since sexual appetite does not spare the decaying body. The pursuit by Lady Wishfort and Lady Touchwood (*The Double Dealer*) of young men borders on dark comedy.

275 green sickness: chlorosis, an anemic disease of young women

276 latter spring: late spring, i.e., a rejuvenation coming too late, introducing autumn or the onset of decay

279 full sail: i.e., like a boat in full sail

280 streamers: flags, i.e., the ribbons of her headdress
shoal: cluster
tenders: attending boats

282 sculler: a small boat

285 beau monde: fashionable company or society
throng: crowd
perukes: wigs

which you have provided for her, I suppose she will submit anything to get rid of him.

MIRABELL.

Yes, I think the good lady would marry anything that resembled a man, though 'twere no more than what a butler could pinch out of a napkin.

MRS. FAINALL.

Female frailty ! We must all come to it, if we live to be old and feel the craving of a false appetite when the true is decayed.

MIRABELL.

An old woman's appetite is depraved like that of a girl. 'Tis the green sickness of a second childhood; and like the faint offer of a latter spring, serves but to usher in the fall, and withers in an affected bloom.

MRS. FAINALL.

Here's your mistress.

Enter Mrs. Millamant, Witwoud *and* Mincing.

MIRABELL.

Here she comes, i'faith, full sail, with her fan spread and her streamers out, and a shoal of fools for tenders. Ha, no, I cry her mercy !

MRS. FAINALL.

I see but one poor empty sculler; and he tows her woman after him.

MIRABELL.

You seem to be unattended, madam. You used to have the beau monde throng after you, and a flock of gay fine perukes hovering round you.

WITWOUD.

Like moths about a candle. I had like to have lost my comparison for want of breath.

MILLAMANT.

Oh, I have denied myself airs today. I have walked as fast through the crowd—

292 similitudes: similes. Witwoud has a tiresome habit of finding similes for everything

306 The vogue of philandering and adultery in upper-class Restoration society. Mirabell indulges in witticism at Witwoud's level.

307 a hit! … hit: a neatly phrased repartee

308 abroad: out

309–310 Millamant's confused manner is partly put-on coquetry.

WITWOUD.

As a favourite in disgrace, and with as few followers.

MILLAMANT.

Dear Mr. Witwoud, truce with your similitudes; for I am as sick of 'em—

WITWOUD.

As a physician of a good air. I cannot help it, madam, though 'tis against myself.

MILLAMANT.

Yet again ! Mincing, stand between me and his wit.

WITWOUD.

Do, Mrs. Mincing, like a screen before a great fire. I confess I do blaze today; I am too bright.

MRS. FAINALL.

But, dear Millamant, why were you so long?

MILLAMANT.

Long ! Lord, have I not made violent haste? I have asked every living thing I met for you; I have inquired after you, as after a new fashion.

WITWOUD.

Madam, truce with your similitudes. No, you met her husband, and did not ask him for her.

MIRABELL.

By your leave, Witwoud, that were like inquiring after an old fashion, to ask a husband for his wife.

WITWOUD.

Hum, a hit ! a hit ! a palpable hit ! I confess it.

MRS. FAINALL.

You were dressed before I came abroad.

MILLAMANT.

Aye, that's true. Oh, but then I had—Mincing, what had I? Why was I so long?

311 mem: madam
la'ship: ladyship
pecquet: packet. Mincing's speech is affected
322 tift: stroked and set (hair)
323 cremp: cramp
326 crips: obsolete form of 'crisp'
329ff Millamant playfully adopts the pose of the conventionally haughty and cruel woman. That the pose does not fit her liberates her from the manipulative stereotype and enlivens the game of courtship.

MINCING.

O mem, your la'ship stayed to peruse a pecquet of letters.

MILLAMANT.

Oh, aye, letters; I had letters. I am persecuted with letters. I hate letters. Nobody knows how to write letters; and yet one has 'em, one does not know why. They serve one to pin up one's hair.

WITWOUD.

Is that the way? Pray, madam, do you pin up your hair with all your letters? I find I must keep copies.

MILLAMANT.

Only with those in verse, Mr. Witwoud. I never pin up my hair with prose. I fancy one's hair would not curl if it were pinned up with prose. I think I tried once, Mincing.

MINCING.

O mem, I shall never forget it.

MILLAMANT.

Aye, poor Mincing tift and tift all the morning.

MINCING.

'Till I had the cremp in my fingers, I'll vow, mem. And all to no purpose. But when your la'ship pins it up with poetry, it sits so pleasant the next day as anything, and is so pure and so crips.

WITWOUD

Indeed, so crips?

MINCING.

You're such a critic, Mr. Witwoud.

MILLAMANT.

Mirabell, did not you take exceptions last night? Oh, aye, and went away. Now I think on't, I'm angry. No, now I think on't, I'm pleased; for I believe I gave you some pain.

MIRABELL.

Does that please you?

342ff The beauty that breeds vanity before the mirror is short-lived and illusory. By contrast, the beauty that is the lover's gift testifies to the humanity, the restorative and renewing power of love

349ff Congreve's triumph lies in his ability to make witty small talk suggest the growth of an abiding passion and affection

357 card-matches: matches made from cardboard

MILLAMANT.

Infinitely; I love to give pain.

MIRABELL.

You would affect a cruelty which is not in your nature; your true vanity is in the power of pleasing.

MILLAMANT.

Oh, I ask your pardon for that. One's cruelty is one's power; and when one parts with one's cruelty, one parts with one's power; and when one has parted with that, I fancy one's old and ugly.

MIRABELL.

Aye, aye suffer your cruelty to ruin the object of your power, to destroy your lover, and then how vain, how lost a thing you'll be! Nay, 'tis true: you are no longer handsome when you've lost your lover; your beauty dies upon the instant. For beauty is the lover's gift; 'tis he bestows your charms, your glass is all a cheat. The ugly and the old, whom the looking glass mortifies, yet after commendation can be flattered by it, and discover beauties in it; for that reflects our praises, rather than your face.

MILLAMANT.

Oh, the vanity of these men ! Fainall, d'ye hear him? If they did not commend us, we were not handsome ! Now you must know they could not commend one, if one was not handsome. Beauty the lover's gift ! Lord, what is a lover, that it can give? Why, one makes lovers as fast as one pleases, and they live as long as one pleases, and they die as soon as one pleases; and then, if one pleases, one makes more.

WITWOUD.

Very pretty. Why, you make no more of making of lovers, madam, than of making so many card-matches.

MILLAMANT.

One no more owes one's beauty to a lover than one's wit to an echo. They can but reflect what we look and say; vain empty things if we are silent or unseen, and want a being.

374 impart: communicate

377–83 Despite the control, Mirabell's emotional involvement brings a different note into the scene.

379 easiness: lenience

379 incumbrance: burden, obstacle

MIRABELL.

Yet to those two vain empty things you owe two [of] the greatest pleasures of your life.

MILLAMANT.

How so?

MIRABELL.

To your lover you owe the pleasure of hearing yourselves praised; and to an echo the pleasure of hearing yourselves talk.

WITWOUD.

But I know a lady that loves talking so incessantly she won't give an echo fair play; she has that everlasting rotation of tongue, that an echo must wait till she dies, before it can catch her last words.

MILLAMANT.

Oh, fiction! Fainall, let us leave these men.

MIRABELL.

Draw off Witwoud. [*Aside to* Mrs. Fainall.]

MRS. FAINALL.

Immediately. I have a word or two for Mr. Witwoud.

Exeunt Witwoud *and* Mrs. Fainall.

MIRABELL.

I would beg a little private audience too. You had the tyranny to deny me last night, though you knew I came to impart a secret to you that concerned my love.

MILLAMANT.

You saw I was engaged.

MIRABELL.

Unkind! You had the leisure to entertain a herd of fools; things who visit you from their excessive idleness, bestowing on your easiness that time which is the incumbrance of their lives. How can you find delight in such society? It is impossible they should admire you; they are not capable. Or if they were, it should be to you as a mortification, for sure to please a fool is some degree of folly.

388 vapours: Such is the boredom peculiar to the life of upper-class women that even the company of fools offers relief from it.
asafoetida: a resinous, medicinal gum with a strong garlic-like smell (commonly used in Indian cooking)

389 a course of fools: company of fools, as medicine for depression

393 physic: art of healing

394 distemper: ailment, disorder

MILLAMANT.

I please myself. Besides, sometimes to converse with fools is for my health.

MIRABELL.

Your health! Is there a worse disease than the conversation of fools?

MILLAMANT.

Yes, the vapours; fools are physic for it, next to asafoetida.

MIRABELL.

You are not in a course of fools?

MILLAMANT.

Mirabell, if you persist in this offensive freedom, you'll displease me. I think I must resolve, after all, not to have you; we shan't agree.

MIRABELL.

Not in our physic, it may be.

MILLAMANT.

And yet our distemper, in all likelihood, will be the same; for we shall be sick of one another. I shan't endure to be reprimanded nor instructed; 'tis so dull to act always by advice, and so tedious to be told of one's faults—I can't bear it. Well, I won't have you, Mirabell—I'm resolved—I think—you may go.—Ha ! ha ! ha ! What would you give that you could help loving me?

MIRABELL.

I would give something that you did not know I could not help it.

MILLAMANT.

Come, don't look grave then. Well, what do you say to me?

MIRABELL.

I say that a man may as soon make a friend by his wit, or a fortune by his honesty, as win a woman with plain dealing and sincerity.

407 sentențious: fond of pompous moralizing, full of maxims. Mirabell's sententiousness is inseparable from his love, the earnestness of which is the subject of Millamant's teasing. This joyous and effervescent banter is reminiscent of the heroines of Shakespearian comedy, with its critique of conventional love and love-sickness

408 Solomon: The famous Biblical story (I Kings 3: 16-28) of two women laying claim to the same child before King Solomon, and the King ordering it to be cut in two to be shared by both. The real mother at once gives up her claim because she does not want her child to die. This ingenious resolution of the dispute was an instance of Solomon's wisdom which became a popular subject for tapestry art.

415 peevish: irritable

Heighho: expression of boredom or disappointment

416 watch-light: night-light or slow-burning candle

428ff The parallel of the whirlwind highlights the incalculable and ungovernable power of passion, thereby challenging the dominant ideology of possessive individualism, of rationalist egoism. The image also admirably captures the procreative urge and fertility-worship that finds its sublimation in love. In keeping with the temper of the age, love is founded upon a reasonable acknowledgement and accommodation of the force of instinct, upon a wisdom that consists in submission to the enactment of folly.

MILLAMANT.

Sententious Mirabell ! Prithee, don't look with that violent and inflexible wise face, like Solomon at the dividing of the child in an old tapestry hanging.

MIRABELL.

You are merry, madam, but I would persuade you for one moment to be serious.

MILLAMANT

What, with that face? No, if you keep your countenance, 'tis impossible I should hold mine. Well, after all, there is something very moving in a love-sick face. Ha ! ha ! ha !—Well, I won't laugh, don't be peevish—Heighho ! Now I'll be melancholy, as melancholy as a watch-light. Well, Mirabell, if ever you will win me, woo me now.—Nay, if you are so tedious, fare you well.—I see they are walking away.

MIRABELL.

Can you not find in the variety of your disposition one moment—

MILLAMANT.

To hear you tell me Foible's married, and your plot like to speed?—No.

MIRABELL.

But how came you to know it?

MILLAMANT.

Unless by the help of the devil, you can't imagine; unless she should tell me herself. Which of the two it may have been, I will leave you to consider; and when you have done thinking of that, think of me. *Exit with* Mincing.

MIRABELL.

I have something more—Gone! Think of you! To think of a whirlwind, though 'twere in a whirlwind, were a case of more steady contemplation; a very tranquility of mind and mansion. A fellow that lives in a windmill has not a more whimsical dwelling than the heart of a man that is lodged in a woman. There is no point of the compass to which they cannot turn,

437 dictates: authoritative directions

438 turtles: turtle doves (believed to be great lovers)
billing: exchanging caresses, kissing

439 Valentine's Day: 14 February, feast day of St. Valentine, patron saint of lovers. On this day, when he was beheaded, birds were supposed to pair

443 solacing: taking pleasure

448 O las: Alas

449 inquietudes: uneasiness

454ff The trap laid for Lady Wishfort makes clever use of the obsolete and spurious convention of Petrarchan love.

457 enamoured of: charmed by

and by which they are not turned; and by one as well as another, for motion, not method, is their occupation. To know this, and yet continue to be in love, is to be made wise from the dictates of reason, and yet persevere to play the fool by the force of instinct.—Oh, here come my pair of turtles!—What, billing so sweetly! Is not Valentine's Day over with you yet?

Enter Waitwell *and* Foible.

Sirrah, Waitwell, why sure you think you were married for your own recreation, and not for my conveniency.

WAITWELL

Your pardon, sir. With submission, we have indeed been solacing in lawful delights; but still with an eye to business, sir. I have instructed her as well as I could. If she can take your directions as readily as my instructions, sir, your affairs are in a prosperous way.

MIRABELL.

Give you joy, Mrs. Foible.

FOIBLE.

O las, sir, I'm so ashamed ! I'm afraid my lady has been in a thousand inquietudes for me. But I protest, sir, I made as much haste as I could.

WAITWELL.

That she did indeed, sir. It was my fault that she did not make more.

MIRABELL.

That I believe.

FOIBLE.

But I told my lady as you instructed me, sir, that I had a prospect of seeing Sir Rowland, your uncle; and I would put her ladyship's picture in my pocket to show him, which I'll be sure to say has made him so enamoured of her beauty, that he burns with impatience to lie at her ladyship's feet and worship the original.

468 spouse: Waitwell as husband tries to claim from Foible the money she receives from Mirabell.
473 toilet: process of dressing
477 B'w'y: contraction of *God be with you* or *Good-bye*
478 jade: (in playful disapproval) woman
pert: forward or saucy in speech and conduct
479 preferment: promotion

MIRABELL.

Excellent Foible! Matrimony has made you eloquent in love.

WAITWELL.

I think she has profited, sir. I think so.

FOIBLE.

You have seen Madam Millamant, sir?

MIRABELL.

Yes.

FOIBLE.

I told her, sir, because I did not know that you might find an opportunity; she had so much company last night.

MIRABELL.

Your diligence will merit more. In the meantime—

Gives money.

FOIBLE.

O dear sir, your humble servant.

WAITWELL.

Spouse.

MIRABELL.

Stand off, sir, not a penny! Go on and prosper, Foible; the lease shall be made good and the farm stocked, if we succeed.

FOIBLE.

I don't question your generosity, sir; and you need not doubt of success. If you have no more commands, sir, I'll be gone; I'm sure my lady is at her toilet and can't dress till I come.— Oh dear, I'm sure that [*looking out*] was Mrs. Marwood that went by in a mask; if she has seen me with you I'm sure she'll tell my lady. I'll make haste home and prevent her. Your servant, sir B'w'y, Waitwell. *Exit.*

WAITWELL.

Sir Rowland, if you please. The jade's so pert upon her preferment she forgets herself.

480 transform: In this world, identities can be put on and taken off like disguises.

483 knighted: made a knight, i.e., honoured with an equivalent rank ('Sir')

MIRABELL.

Come, sir, will you endeavour to forget yourself, and transform into Sir Rowland?

WAITWELL.

Why, sir, it will be impossible I should remember myself. Married, knighted, and attended all in one day ! 'Tis enough to make any man forget himself. The difficulty will be how to recover my acquaintance and familiarity with my former self, and fall from my transformation to a reformation into Waitwell. Nay, I shan't be quite the same Waitwell neither; for now I remember me, I am married and can't be my own man again.

Aye, there's the grief; that's the sad change of life,
To lose my title, and yet keep my wife. *Exeunt.*

[III]

1 Merciful!: ie, Merciful Heaven

3 fretted: worried, tormented

4 veracity: truth

4 red: colour of make-up

5 arrant: entirely

6 person: person of distinction

7 mopus: idiot

10 Spanish paper: a variety of Spanish rouge

13 wooden ...wires: puppet

18–19 Mrs Qualmsick ... breeding: a reference to the local priest's wife whose weakness and pallor are caused by continuous child-bearing Her name ('Qualm') indicates her religious background

Act III, Scene I

A *Room in* Lady Wishfort's *House.*
Lady Wishfort *at her toilet,* Peg *waiting.*

LADY WISHFORT.
Merciful ! no news of Foible yet?

PEG.
No, madam.

LADY WISHFORT.
I have no more patience. If I have not fretted myself till I am pale again, there's no veracity in me ! Fetch me the red; the red, do you hear, sweetheart? An arrant ash colour, as I'm a person ! Look you how this wench stirs ! Why dost thou not fetch me a little red? Didst thou not hear me, mopus?

PEG.
The red ratafia does your ladyship mean, or the cherry brandy?

LADY WISHFORT.
Ratafia, fool ! No, fool ! Not the ratafia, fool. Grant me patience! I mean the Spanish paper, idiot; complexion, darling. Paint, paint, paint, dost thou understand that, changeling, dangling thy hands like bobbins before thee? Why dost thou not stir, puppet? thou wooden thing upon wires ?

PEG.
Lord, madam, your ladyship is so impatient. I cannot come at the paint, madam; Mrs. Foible has locked it up and carried the key with her.

LADY WISHFORT.
A pox take you both ! Fetch me the cherry brandy then. (*Exit* Peg.) I'm as pale and as faint, I look like Mrs. Qualmsick, the curate's wife, that's always breeding. Wench, come, come, wench, what art thou doing? Sipping? Tasting? Save thee, dost thou not know the bottle?

Re-enter Peg *with a bottle and china cup.*

PEG.
Madam, I was looking for a cup.

24 acorn: fruit of the oak tree (shaped like a thimble)
25 thimble: metal cup worn on finger to protect it during sewing
25 brass thimble …nutmeg: as good luck charms
30 tapster: barmaid or barman
31–32 Maritornes the Asturian: an ugly chambermaid who brings water to revive Sancho in Cervantes' *Don Quixote*
35 dishabillé: being partly or improperly dressed
42 durst: past tense or conditional tense of 'dare'
44 wheedling: persuading or cheating by flattery
wrought: worked

LADY WISHFORT.

A cup, save thee! and what a cup hast thou brought ! Dost thou take me for a fairy, to drink out of an acorn? Why didst thou not bring thy thimble? Hast thou ne'er a brass thimble clinking in thy pocket with a bit of nutmeg? I warrant thee. Come, fill, fill ! So; again.

[*One knocks.*]

See who that is. Set down the bottle first. Here, here, under the table. What, wouldst thou go with the bottle in thy hand, like a tapster? As I'm a person, this wench has lived in an inn upon the road, before she came to me like Maritornes the Asturian in *Don Quixote* ! No Foible yet?

PEG.

No madam, Mrs. Marwood.

LADY WISHFORT.

Oh, Marwood, let her come in. Come in, good Marwood.

Enter Mrs. Marwood.

MRS. MARWOOD.

I'm surprised to find your ladyship in dishabillé at this time of day.

LADY WISHFORT.

Foible's a lost thing ; has been abroad since morning, and never heard of since.

MRS. MARWOOD.

I saw her but now, as I came masked through the park, in conference with Mirabell.

LADY WISHFORT.

With Mirabell ! You call my blood into my face with mentioning that traitor. She durst not have the confidence ! I sent her to negotiate an affair in which, if I'm detected, I'm undone. If that wheedling villain has wrought upon Foible to detect me, I'm ruined. Oh my dear friend, I'm a wretch of wretches if I'm detected.

MRS. MARWOOD.

O madam, you cannot suspect Mrs. Foible's integrity.

53 closet: small private room

55 Quarles: Francis Quarles, seventeenth-century religious poet

55 Prynne: William Prynne, seventeenth-century Puritan author

Short View of the Stage: *A Short View of the Immorality and Profaneness of the English Stage* by Jeremy Collier, published in 1698, two years before *The Way of the World*, had attacked Congreve's comedies

56 Bunyan's works: Famous for his allegory *The Pilgrim's Progress* (1678–79), Bunyan was a popular Puritan writer In *The Old Bachelor*, Congreve had ridiculed Puritan values

Lady Wishfort's choice of books is related to her view on her daughter's education (see Act V, ii 168–80), dictated by hypocrisy and sanctimoniousness

61 transported: carried away by strong emotion

63 if worshipping … sin: the worship of religious images in Roman Catholic churches was sinful in the eyes of Anglicans and Puritans

64 miniature: a small-scale portrait

64 like: i.e., as a likeness

65 detected: exposed

68ff Foible's quick practical intelligence not only places her in a long line of servant-knaves in comic drama but also reinforces the war of wits that is central to the play

LADY WISHFORT.

Oh, he carries poison in his tongue that would corrupt integrity itself! If she has given him an opportunity, she has as good as put her integrity into his hands. Ah, dear Marwood, what's integrity to an opportunity? Hark! I hear her! Go, you thing, and send her in. [*Exit* Peg.] Dear friend, retire into my closet, that I may examine her with more freedom. You'll pardon me, dear friend; I can make bold with you. There are books over the chimney. Quarles and Prynne, and the *Short View of the Stage*, with Bunyan's works, to entertain you.

Exit Mrs. Marwood.

O Foible, where hast thou been? What hast thou been doing?

FOIBLE.

Madam, I have seen the party.

LADY WISHFORT.

But what hast thou done?

FOIBLE.

Nay, 'tis your ladyship has done, and are to do; I have only promised. But a man so enamoured, so transported! Well, here it is, all that is left; all that is not kissed away. Well, if worshipping of pictures be a sin, poor Sir Rowland, I say.

LADY WISHFORT.

The miniature has been counted like. But hast thou not betrayed me, Foible? Hast thou not detected me to that faithless Mirabell? What hadst thou to do with him in the Park? Answer me, has he got nothing out of thee?

FOIBLE [*aside*].

So the devil has been beforehand with me. What shall I say? —Alas, madam, could I help it, if I met that confident thing? Was I in fault? If you had heard how he used me, and all upon your ladyship's account, I'm sure you would not suspect my fidelity. Nay, if that had been the worst, I could have borne; but he had a fling at your ladyship too. And then I could not hold; but i'faith I gave him his own.

77 fleers: mocking looks or speech
79 catering: procuring
ferreting: searching
disbanded: dispersed
80 subsistence: livelihood
82 superannuated: declared too old for work or utility
84 Ods: *God's*
85 drawer: waiter
86 Locket's: popular tavern in London
94 fit: punish
96 frippery: old, ragged clothes

LADY WISHFORT.

Me? What did the filthy fellow say?

FOIBLE.

O madam ! 'tis a shame to say what he said, with his taunts and his fleers, tossing up his nose. Humph ! (says he), what, you are a hatching some plot (says he), you are so early abroad, or catering (says he), ferreting for some disbanded officer, I warrant. Half-pay is but thin subsistence (says he). Well, what pension does your lady propose? Let me see (says he), what, she must come down pretty deep now, she's superannuated (says he) and—

LADY WISHFORT.

Ods my life, I'll have him, I'll have him murdered. I'll have him poisoned. Where does he eat? I'll marry a drawer to have him poisoned in his wine. I'll send for Robin from Locket's immediately.

FOIBLE.

Poison him? Poisoning's too good for him. Starve him, madam, starve him; marry Sir Rowland and get him disinherited. Oh, you would bless yourself to hear what he said !

LADY WISHFORT.

A villain ! superannuated !

FOIBLE.

Humph ! (says he), I hear you are laying designs against me too (says he), and Mrs. Millamant is to marry my uncle (he does not suspect a word of your ladyship); but (says he) I'll fit you for that. I warrant you (says he), I'll hamper you for that (says he), you and your old frippery too (says he), I'll handle you—

LADY WISHFORT.

Audacious villain ! Handle me ! would he durst ! Frippery ? old frippery ! Was there ever such a foulmouthed fellow? I'll be married tomorrow; I'll be contracted tonight.

FOIBLE.

The sooner the better, madam.

102 incontinently: at once
107 tatterdemalion: person in tattered clothes
108 Long Lane penthouse: Long Lane was known for its rag-sellers whose stalls may have been set up under the overhanging roofs of houses (penthouse)
109 gibbet: upright post with arm on which criminals were hanged to death
railer: one who uses abusive language
110 million lottery: the government lottery of 1694 to raise a million pounds This was the age of the National Debt.
111 court ... birthday: Courtiers ran into debts trying to buy new and expensive clothes on the King's birthday.
114 Ludgate: mainly a debtor's prison
114–115 angle ... mitten: The prisoners would 'fish' for alms with a mitten let down on a line from upper windows to passers-by in the street. Brass farthings were the smallest units of money.
117ff Lady Wishfort's prosthetic toilet is a comment on the undignified vying for male attention that characterizes the life of women in Restoration society.
118 economy: orderly arrangement
119 decayed: the references are to the spoiling of her make-up
123 flayed: skinned (since the paint is a layer of her skin)
peeled wall: wall whose paint is falling of
127–128 Life imitating art is an apt comment on fashionable Restoration society.

LADY WISHFORT.

Will Sir Rowland be here, say'st thou? When, Foible?

FOIBLE.

Incontinently, madam. No new sheriff's wife expects the return of her husband after knighthood with that impatience in which Sir Rowland burns for the dear hour of kissing your ladyship's hands after dinner.

LADY WISHFORT.

Frippery? superannuated frippery! I'll frippery the villain; I'll reduce him to frippery and rags ! A tatterdemalion I hope to see him hung with tatters, like a Long Lane penthouse or a gibbet thief. A slander-mouthed railer ! I warrant the spendthrift prodigal's in debt as much as the million lottery, or the whole court upon a birthday. I'll spoil his credit with his tailor. Yes, he shall have my niece with her fortune, he shall !

FOIBLE.

He ! I hope to see him lodge in Ludgate first, and angle into Blackfriars for brass farthings with an old mitten.

LADY WISHFORT.

Aye, dear Foible; thank thee for that, dear Foible. He has put me out of all patience. I shall never recompose my features to receive Sir Rowland with any economy of face. This wretch has fretted me that I am absolutely decayed. Look, Foible.

FOIBLE.

Your ladyship has frowned a little too rashly, indeed, madam. There are some cracks discernible in the white varnish.

LADY WISHFORT.

Let me see the glass. Cracks, say'st thou? Why I am arrantly flayed; I look like an old peeled wall. Thou must repair me, Foible, before Sir Rowland comes, or I shall never keep up to my picture.

FOIBLE.

I warrant you, madam, a little art once made your picture like you; and now a little of the same art must make you like your picture. Your picture must sit for you, madam.

130 importunate: persistent, forward

132 decorums: rules of polite behaviour (cp 'forms' in 1396)

134ff The parody of the arts and anxieties of decorous courtship holds a precarious balance between farce and cruelty

137 amiss: inappropriate

139 dyingness: exaggerated show of softness or weakness

140 swimmingness: dreaminess

141 affects: tries to put on or imitate

141 wants: lacks

146 brisk: lively and bold

LADY WISHFORT.

But art thou sure Sir Rowland will not fail to come? Or will he not fail when he does come? Will he be importunate, Foible, and push? For if he should not be importunate, I shall never break decorums. I shall die with confusion, if I am forced to advance. Oh no, I can never advance! I shall swoon if he should expect advances. No, I hope Sir Rowland is better bred than to put a lady to the necessity of breaking her forms. I won't be too coy neither. I won't give him despair; but a little disdain is not amiss, a little scorn is alluring.

FOIBLE.

A little scorn becomes your ladyship.

LADY WISHFORT.

Yes, but tenderness becomes me best, a sort of a dyingness. You see that picture has a sort of a—ha, Foible? A swimmingness in the eyes. Yes, I'll look so. My niece affects it; but she wants features. Is Sir Rowland handsome? Let my toilet be removed. I'll dress above. I'll receive Sir Rowland here. Is he handsome? Don't answer me. I won't know; I'll be surprised, I'll be taken by surprise.

FOIBLE.

By storm, madam. Sir Rowland's a brisk man.

LADY WISHFORT.

Is he ! Oh, then he'll importune; if he's a brisk man. I shall save decorums if Sir Rowland importunes. I have a mortal terror at the apprehension of offending against decorums. Nothing but importunity can surmount decorums. Oh, I'm glad he's a brisk man. Let my things be removed, good Foible. *Exit.*

Enter Mrs. Fainall.

MRS. FAINALL.

O Foible, I have been in fright, lest I should come too late ! That devil Marwood saw you in the Park with Mirabell, and I'm afraid will discover it to my lady.

164 correspondence: relationship

167 winning: able to win people over

168 pattern of generosity: Since Foible does not attempt to flatter, her praise is that of the dramatist as well.

177 Welsh maidenhead: The readiness of Welsh maidams to give up their virginity was perhaps a commonplace resulting from racial subjugation by the English.

182 month's mind: liking for Mirabell

182 abide: tolerate

FOIBLE.

Discover what, madam?

MRS. FAINALL.

Nay, nay put not on that strange face. I am privy to the whole design, and know that Waitwell, to whom thou wert this morning married, is to personate Mirabell's uncle, and as such, winning my lady, to involve her in those difficulties from which Mirabell only must release her, by his making his conditions to have my cousin and her fortune left to her own disposal.

FOIBLE.

O dear madam, I beg your pardon. It was not my confidence in your ladyship that was deficient; but I thought the former good correspondence between your ladyship and Mr. Mirabell might have hindered his communicating this secret.

MRS. FAINALL.

Dear Foible, forget that.

FOIBLE.

O dear madam, Mr. Mirabell is such a sweet, winning gentleman, but your ladyship is the pattern of generosity. Sweet lady, to be so good! Mr. Mirabell cannot choose but be grateful. I find your ladyship has his heart still. Now, madam, I can safely tell your ladyship our success. Mrs. Marwood had told my lady; but I warrant I managed myself. I turned it all for the better. I told my lady that Mr. Mirabell railed at her. I laid horrid things to this charge, I'll vow; and my lady is so incensed that she'll be contracted to Sir Rowland tonight, she says. I warrant I worked her up, that he may have her for asking for, as they say of a Welsh maidenhead.

MRS. FAINALL.

O rare Foible !

FOIBLE.

Madam, I beg your ladyship to acquaint Mr. Mirabell of his success. I would be seen as little as possible to speak to him; besides, I believe Madam Marwood watches me. She has a month's mind; but I know Mr. Mirabell can't abide her.

183 my lady's: Lady Wishfort's
187 Mrs Engine: Mrs Ingenious
189 *passe-partout*: master key, key that opens all doors in a building
190 strongbox: burglar-proof box for keeping valuables
191 swimmingly: with easy and unobstructed progress
193 surfeit: excess of pleasure causing loss of appetite
194 procure: to get a woman (for Mirabell)
198 driveller: one who talks idiotically or childishly; also runs at the mouth or nose
198 bells: a fool's cap and bells
horns: referring to the horns of a cuckold
201 confessor: one (especially priest) who hears confessions
202 without you ... closer: without your being able to keep his secret
203 stalk for him: pursue stealthily (to help Mirabell in hunting down Millamant and her fortune)
207 chemist: alchemist
208 projection: the final stage in alchemical transmutation of base metal into gold See Ben Jonson's *The Alchemist*

[*Enter* Footman.] John, remove my lady's toilet. Madam, your servant. My lady is so impatient, I fear she'll come for me, if I stay.

MRS. FAINALL.
I'll go with you up the backstairs, lest I should meet her.
Exeunt.

Enter Mrs. Marwood.

MRS. MARWOOD.
Indeed, Mrs. Engine, is it thus with you? Are you become a go-between of this importance? Yes, I shall watch you. Why this wench is the *passe-partout,* a very master key to everybody's strongbox. My friend Fainall, have you carried it so swimmingly? I thought there was something in it; but it seems it's over with you. Your loathing is not from a want of appetite then, but from surfeit. Else you could never be so cool to fall from a principal to be an assistant; to procure for him! A pattern of generosity, that I confess. Well, Mr. Fainall, you have met with your match. O man, man! woman, woman! The devil's an ass; if I were a painter, I would draw him like an idiot, a driveller with a bib and bells. Man should have his head and horns, and woman the rest of him. Poor simple fiend! Madam Marwood has a month's mind, but he can't abide her. 'Twere better for him you had not been his confessor in that affair, without you could have kept his counsel closer. I shall not prove another pattern of generosity and stalk for him, till he takes his stand to aim at a fortune. He has not obliged me to that, with those excesses of himself; and now I'll have none of him. Here comes the good lady, panting ripe; with a heart full of hope, and a head full of care, like any chemist upon the day of projection.

Enter Lady Wishfort.

LADY WISHFORT.
O dear Marwood, what shall I say, for this rude forgetfulness? But my dear friend is all goodness.

MRS. MARWOOD.
No apologies, dear madam. I have been very well entertained.

213 olio: a Spanish or Portuguese stew with many ingredients; hence, a hodgepodge

216 travel for improvement: Travel or the Grand Tour of the Continent, indispensable to a gentleman's education, had already begun to be debased by social mobility. See Pope's *The Dimciad.*

LADY WISHFORT.

As I'm a person, I am in a very chaos to think I should so forget myself; but I have such an olio of affairs, really I know not what to do. [*Calls.*] Foible !—I expect my nephew, Sir Wilfull, every moment too.—Why, Foible !—He means to travel for improvement.

MRS. MARWOOD.

Methinks Sir Wilfull should rather think of marrying than travelling at his years. I hear he is turned of forty.

LADY WISHFORT.

Oh, he's in less danger of being spoiled by his travels. I am against my nephew's marrying too young. It will be time enough when he comes back and has acquired discretion to choose for himself.

MRS. MARWOOD.

Methinks Mrs. Millamant and he would make a very fit match. He may travel afterwards. 'Tis a thing very usual with young gentlemen.

LADY WISHFORT.

I promise you I have thought on't; and since 'tis your judgment, I'll think on't again. I assure you I will; I value your judgment extremely. On my word, I'll propose it.

Enter Foible.

Come, come, Foible, I had forgot my nephew will be here before dinner. I must make haste.

FOIBLE.

Mr. Witwoud and Mr. Petulant are come to dine with your ladyship.

LADY WISHFORT.

Oh dear, I can't appear till I'm dressed. Dear Marwood, shall I be free with you again, and beg you to entertain 'em? I'll make all imaginable haste. Dear friend, excuse me.

Exeunt Lady Wishfort *and* Foible.

237 You have a colour: referring to her flushed face

240 powder: powdering hair was fashionable
fit: fought (in Mincing's affected pronunciation)

246ff The freedom that women have is to choose their clothes but not their company The implied equivalence of 'clothes' and 'companions' is carried on wittily

251 doily stuff: cheap woollen fabric

253 wear ... wear: the first 'wear' refers to putting on clothes, the second to the damage they suffer by usage

254 *drap-de-Berry*: coarse woollen cloth from France
The scene between the two women brings to the surface a continuous undercurrent of suspicion and hostility originating in competition for the love of Mirabell

Enter Mrs. Millamant *and* Mincing.

MILLAMANT.

Sure never anything was so unbred as that odious man! Marwood, your servant.

MRS. MARWOOD.

You have a colour, what's the matter?

MILLAMANT.

That horrid fellow, Petulant, has provoked me into a flame. I have broken my fan. Mincing, lend me yours; is not all the powder out of my hair?

MRS. MARWOOD.

No, what has he done?

MILLAMANT.

Nay, he has done nothing; he has only talked. Nay he has said nothing neither; but he has contradicted everything that has been said. For my part, I thought Witwoud and he would have quarrelled.

MINCING.

I vow, mem, I thought once they would have fit.

MILLAMANT.

Well, 'tis a lamentable thing, I'll swear, that one has not the liberty of choosing one's acquaintance as one does one's clothes.

MRS. MARWOOD.

If we had the liberty, we should be as weary of one set of acquaintance, though never so good, as we are of one suit, though never so fine. A fool and a doily stuff would now and then find days of grace, and be worn for variety.

MILLAMANT.

I could consent to wear 'em, if they would wear alike; but fools never wear out—they are such *drap-de-Berry* things without one could give 'em to one's chambermaid after a day or two!

MRS. MARWOOD.

'Twere better so indeed. Or what think you of the playhouse?

259 habit: costume
259 masquerade: masked ball
261 blind: cover up
266 Mrs Primly: the name suggests prim manners
267 burnishes: grows plump
268 Strammel: a lean, gaunt, ill-favoured person
goodly: handsome (ironic)
269–270 Rhenish wine tea: strong wine (from the Rhine valley in Germany) instead of tea White Rhenish wine was believed to reduce obesity and flushed complexion Alternatively, thin tea coloured like white Rhenish wine may be meant
270 comprehended: contained
271 I'll take my death: equivalent to 'I swear'
272 discarded toast: person who has lost popularity and hence whose health is no longer drunk
279 nettled: irritated
285 enjoined: commanded, instructed

A fine, gay, glossy fool should be given there, like a new masking habit, after the masquerade is over, and we have done with the disguise. For a fool's visit is always a disguise, and never admitted by a woman of wit, but to blind her affair with a lover of sense. If you would but appear barefaced now, and own Mirabell, you might as easily put off Petulant and Witwoud as your hood and scarf. And indeed 'tis time, for the town has found it; the secret is grown too big for the pretence. 'Tis like Mrs. Primly's great belly; she may lace it down before, but it burnishes on her hips. Indeed, Millamant, you can no more conceal it than my Lady Strammel can her face, that goodly face, which, in defiance of her Rhenish wine tea, will not be comprehended in a mask.

MILLAMANT.

I'll take my death, Marwood, you are more censorious than a decayed beauty, or a discarded toast. Mincing, tell the men they may come up. My aunt is not dressing [here].—Their folly is less provoking than your malice. [*Exit* Mincing.] The town has found it ! What has it found? That Mirabell loves me is no more a secret than it is a secret that you discovered it to my aunt, or than the reason why you discovered it is a secret.

MRS. MARWOOD.

You are nettled.

MILLAMANT.

You're mistaken. Ridiculous !

MRS. MARWOOD.

Indeed, my dear, you'll tear another fan, if you don't mitigate those violent airs.

MILLAMANT.

O silly ! Ha ! ha ! ha ! I could laugh immoderately. Poor Mirabell ! His constancy to me has quite destroyed his complaisance for all the world beside. I swear, I never enjoined it him to be so coy. If I had the vanity to think he would obey me, I would command him to show more gallantry. 'Tis hardly well-bred to be so particular on one hand, and so insensible

291	barbarous: ill-mannered
294	unhappily: unfortunately
294	miscarry: miss the mark
295–96	I did not mind you: Millamant claims that she was unmindful
302	forbear: refrain from
303	sybil: pagan prophetess or sorceress
311	comb: tidy their wigs

on the other. But I despair to prevail, and so let him follow his own way. Ha ! ha ! ha ! Pardon me, dear creature, I must laugh, ha ! ha ! ha !—though I grant you 'tis a little barbarous, ha ! ha ! ha !.

MRS. MARWOOD.

What pity 'tis, so much fine raillery, and delivered with so significant gesture, should be so unhappily directed to miscarry.

MILLAMANT.

Ha? Dear creature, I ask your pardon. I swear I did not mind you.

MRS. MARWOOD.

Mr. Mirabell and you both may think it a thing impossible, when I shall tell him by telling you—

MILLAMANT.

Oh dear, what? For it is the same thing, if I hear it, ha ! ha ! ha !

MRS. MARWOOD.

That I detest him, hate him, madam.

MILLAMANT.

O madam, why so do I—and yet the creature loves me ha ! ha ! ha ! How can one forbear laughing to think it ! I am a sybil if I am not amazed to think what he can see in me. I'll take my death, I think you are handsomer—and within a year or two as young. If you could but stay for me, I should overtake you—but that cannot be.—Well, that thought makes me melancholy.—Now I'll be sad.

MRS. MARWOOD.

Your merry note may be changed sooner than you think.

MILLAMANT.

D'ye say so? Then I'm resolved to have a song to keep up my spirits.

Enter Mincing.

MINCING.

The gentlemen stay but to comb, madam, and will wait on you.

312 Mrs Hodgson: She had a high reputation as a singer

Stage Direction: John Eccles: John Eccles (1650–1735) composed songs for many plays, including Congreve's *Love for Love* and *The Way of the World*

316ff The theme of the song—the triumphant conquest of a man coveted by many women—is particularly appropriate not only to the sexual rivalry of women but also Millamant's conquest of Mirabell.

320 wanton: wild, licentious

322 pierced: wounded in love

swain: young rustic (often lover in the pastoral tradition)

328 animosity composed: hostility pacified

331 in the main: mainly. Also the mean between treble and bass

332 treble and bass: in music, high-pitched and low-pitched, related through the concept of harmony

MILLAMANT.

Desire Mrs.—, that is in the next room, to sing the song I would have learned yesterday. You shall hear it, madam, not that there's any great matter in it, but 'tis agreeable to my humour.

Song

Set by Mr. John Eccles *and sung* by Mrs Hodgson.

I

Love's but the frailty of the mind,
When 'tis not with ambition joined;
A sickly flame, which, if not fed, expires,
And feeding, wastes in self-consuming fires.

II

'Tis not to wound a wanton boy
Or amorous youth, that gives the joy;
But 'tis the glory to have pierced a swain,
For whom inferior beauties signed in vain.

III

Then I alone the conquest prize,
When I insult a rival's eyes;
If there's delight in love, 'tis when I see
The heart, which others bleed for, bleed for me.

Enter Petulant *and* Witwoud.

MILLAMANT.

Is your animosity composed, gentlemen?

WITWOUD.

Raillery, raillery, madam; we have no animosity. We hit off a little wit now and then, but no animosity. The falling-out of wits is like the falling-out of lovers; we agree in the main, like treble and bass. Ha, Petulant?

PETULANT.

Aye, in the main, but when I have a humour to contradict.

WITWOUD.

Aye, when he has a humour to contradict, then I contradict too. What, I know my cue. Then we contradict one another

336 battledores: wooden, stringed, or parchmented bats used with shuttlecock in a game akin to badminton

337 like Jews: a racist reference to the supposed fertility of the Jews

343 proof presumptive: Petulant and Witwoud indulge in pointless and trite logical distinctions, revealing the common folly of pedantry.

349–501 parts: natural talents

like two battledores; for contradictions beget one another like Jews.

PETULANT.

If he says black's black, if I have a humour to say 'tis blue, let that pass; all's one for that. If I have a humour to prove it, it must be granted.

WITWOUD.

Not positively must, but it may, it may.

PETULANT.

Yes, it positively must, upon proof positive.

WITWOUD.

Aye, upon proof positive it must; but upon proof presumptive it only may. That's a logical distinction now, madam.

MRS. MARWOOD.

I perceive your debates are of importance and very learnedly handled.

PETULANT.

Importance is one thing, and learning's another; but a debate's a debate, that I assert.

WITWOUD.

Petulant's an enemy to learning; he relies altogether on his parts.

PETULANT.

No, I'm no enemy to learning; it hurts not me.

MRS. MARWOOD.

That's a sign indeed it's no enemy to you.

PETULANT.

No, no, it's no enemy to anybody but them that have it.

MILLAMANT.

Well, an illiterate man's my aversion. I wonder at the impudence of any illiterate man to offer to make love.

WITWOUD.

That I confess I wonder at too.

360 The ordinary's … psalm: 'Ordinary' referred to a clergyman. Condemned criminals were ministered to by a clergyman (the Newgate chaplain). Hence Petulant's parallel between marriage and hanging

364 Bartlemew and his fair: Bartholomew Fair was a popular fair held at Smithfield on St Bartholomew's Day, 24 August. As Jonson's comedy of the same name shows, the fair had many strange exhibits to offer and this may be in Witwoud's mind as he looks at Sir Wilfull

367 The Revolution: the Glorious Revolution of 1688 in which the Whigs invited William and Mary to the English throne to begin a new era of constitutional monarchy

368ff The entry of Sir Wilfull Witwoud introduces the values of Shropshire into the totally different milieu of London. The increasing polarization of town and country, vividly presented in *The Spectator* and manifest even in the ideology of the Country party led by Bolingbroke, divides the two brothers, Witwoud and Wilfull, breeding mutual contempt. Sir Wilfull's blunt, affable, even coarse manner contrasts with the foppish airs of Witwoud. Despite the boorishness and illiteracy characterising country life, its frankness and spontaneity constitute a critique of an urban sophistication that represses emotions in subservience to decorum. Witwoud is exposed as a social climber whose aspirations are evident in his false wit, foppish clothes and ornate use of language, oral or written

372 belike: perhaps

MILLAMANT.

Ah! to marry an ignorant that can hardly read or write !

PETULANT.

Why should a man be ever the further from being married, though he can't read, any more than he is from being hanged? The ordinary's paid for setting the psalm, and the parish priest for reading the ceremony. And for the rest which is to follow in both cases, a man may do it without books; so all's one for that.

MILLAMANT.

D'ye hear the creature? Lord, here's company, I'll be gone.

Exeunt Millamant *and* Mincing.

WITWOUD.

In the name of Bartlemew and his fair, what have we here?

MRS. MARWOOD.

'Tis your brother, I fancy. Don't you know him?

WITWOUD.

Not I. Yes, I think it is he. I've almost forgot him; I have not seen him since the Revolution.

Enter Sir Wilfull Witwoud *in a country riding habit, and a* Servant *to* Lady Wishfort.

SERVANT.

Sir, my lady's dressing. Here's company; if you please to walk in, in the meantime.

SIR WILFULL.

Dressing ! What, it's but morning here, I warant, with you in London; we should count it towards afternoon in our parts, down in Shropshire. Why then, belike my aunt han't dined yet, ha, friend?

SERVANT.

Your aunt, sir?

SIR WILFULL.

My aunt, sir ! Yes, my aunt, sir, and your lady, sir; your lady is my aunt, sir. Why, what, dost thou not know me, friend?

383 her face: Lady Wishfort's face, that is, her identity is dependent on her make-up.

386 prithee: please

394 Oons: *God's wounds*

starling: a bird

396 behindhand: slow

Why then, send somebody here that does. How long hast thou lived with thy lady, fellow, ha?

SERVANT.

A week, sir; longer than anybody in the house, except my lady's woman.

SIR WILFULL.

Why then, belike thou dost not know thy lady, if thou seest her, ha, friend?

SERVANT.

Why truly, sir, I cannot safely swear to her face in a morning, before she is dressed. 'Tis like I may give a shrewd guess at her by this time.

SIR WILFULL

Well, prithee try what thou canst do; if thou canst not guess, inquire her out, dost hear, fellow? And tell her, her nephew, Sir Wilfull Witwoud, is in the house.

SERVANT.

I shall, sir.

SIR WILFULL.

Hold ye, hear me, friend; a word with you in your ear. Prithee who are these gallants?

SERVANT.

Really, sir, I can't tell; here come so many here, 'tis hard to know 'em all.

Exit Servant.

SIR WILFULL.

Oons, this fellow knows less than a starling; I don't think a' knows his own name.

MRS. MARWOOD.

Mr. Witwoud, your brother is not behindhand in forgetfulness; I fancy he has forgot you too.

WITWOUD.

I hope so. The devil take him that remembers first, I say.

407 smoke him: make fun of him
412 thereafter: depending on what is meant
413 information … boots: what can be inferred from the condition of the boots

SIR WILFULL.
Save you, gentlemen and lady!

MRS. MARWOOD.
For shame, Mr. Witwoud; why won't you speak to him? And you, sir.

WITWOUD.
Petulant, speak.

PETULANT.
And you, sir.

SIR WILFULL.
No offence, I hope.

Salutes Marwood.

MRS. MARWOOD.
No sure, sir.

WITWOUD.
This is a vile dog, I see that already. No offence! Ha! ha! ha! to him; to him, Petulant, smoke him.

PETULANT.
It seems as if you had come a journey, sir; hem, hem.

Surveying him round.

SIR WILFULL.
Very likely, sir, that it may seem so.

PETULANT.
No offence, I hope, sir.

WITWOUD.
Smoke the boots, the boots; Petulant, the boots ha! ha! ha!

SIR WILFULL.
May be not, sir; thereafter as 'tis meant, sir.

PETULANT.
Sir, I presume upon the information of your boots.

419 'Slife: *God's life*
429 'Sheart: *God's heart*
430 Wrekin: a famous high hill in Shropshire
432–33 be-cravated and be-periwigged: dressed up in necktie and wig (sarcastic)
434 Odso: *Godso*, an expression of surprise
437 flapdragon: something useless
437–38 hare's scut: hare's tail

SIR WILFULL.

Why, 'tis like you may, sir. If you are not satisfied with the information of my boots, sir, if you will step to the stable, you may inquire further of my horse, sir.

PETULANT.

Your horse, sir ! Your horse is an ass, sir !

SIR WILFULL.

Do you speak by way of offence, sir?

MRS. MARWOOD.

The gentleman's merry, that's all, sir—[*Aside*] 'Slife, we shall have a quarrel betwixt an horse and an ass, before they find one another out.—[*Aloud.*] You must not take anything amiss from your friends, sir. You are among your friends here, though it may be you don't know it. If I am not mistaken, you are Sir Wilfull Witwoud.

SIR WILFULL.

Right, lady; I am Sir Wilfull Witwoud, so I write myself; no offence to anybody, I hope; and nephew to the Lady Wishfort of this mansion.

MRS. MARWOOD.

Don't you know this gentleman, sir?

SIR WILFULL.

Hum! What, sure 'tis not—yea by'r Lady, but 'tis. 'Sheart, I know not whether 'tis or no. Yea, but 'tis, by the Wrekin. Brother Anthony! What, Tony, i'faith! What, dost thou not know me? By'r Lady nor I thee, thou art so be-cravated and be-periwigged. 'Sheart, why dost not speak? Art thou o'erjoyed?

WITWOUD.

Odso, brother, is it you? Your servant, brother.

SIR WILFULL.

Your servant ! Why, yours, sir. Your servant again, 'sheart, and your friend and servant to that, and a—[*puff*] and flapdragon for your service, sir ! and a hare's foot, and a hare's scut for your service, sir, an you be so cold and so courtly!

441 Inns o' Court: Inns of Court: four legal societies in London having exclusive right of admitting persons to practise at the bar

443 Salop: Shropshire
short: crumbling (as in shortbread)

444 Shrewsbury cake: a cake characteristic of Shrewsbury, the county town of Shropshire

444 modish: fashionable

446 lubberly: big, clumsy and stupid
slabber: slobber, ie, to wet or drip with saliva

447 call of serjeants: a group of lawyers who were all admitted to the profession at the same time

453 subpoena: writ issued by the court commanding the presence of a defendant to answer the charge against him

455 Rat me: *May God rot me*

456 debauch: bout of sensual indulgence
ods heart: *God's heart*

458 before … time: while you were still indentured (bound as an apprentice) to an attorney

459 Pumple: pimple

459 Furnivall's Inn: an Inn of Court
entreat: request

461 gazettes: news sheets
Dawk's Letter: a newspaper

462 Weekly Bill: weekly record of deaths in London

WITWOUD.

No offence, I hope, brother.

SIR WILFULL.

'Sheart, sir, but there is, and much offence! A pox, is this your Inns o' Court breeding, not to know your friends and your relations, your elders and your betters?

WITWOUD.

Why, brother Wilfull of Salop, you may be as short as a Shrewsbury cake, if you please. But I tell you, 'tis not modish to know relations in town. You think you're in the country, where great lubberly brothers slabber and kiss one another when they meet, like a call of serjeants. 'Tis not the fashion here; 'tis not indeed, dear brother.

SIR WILFULL.

The fashion's a fool; and you're a fop, dear brother. 'Sheart, I've suspected this. By'r Lady, I conjectured you were a fox, since you began to change the style of your letters and write in a scrap of paper, gilt round the edges, no broader than a subpoena. I might expect this when you left off Honoured Brother, and hoping you are in good health, and so forth—to begin with a Rat me, knight, I'm so sick of a last night's debauch—ods heart, and then tell a familiar tale of a cock and a bull, and a whore and a bottle and so conclude. You could write news before you were out of your time, when you lived with honest Pumple Nose, the attorney of Furnival's Inn; you could entreat to be remembered then to your friends round the Wrekin. We could have gazettes then, and *Dawk's Letter,* and the *Weekly Bill,* till of late days.

PETULANT.

'Slife, Witwoud, were you ever an attorney's clerk? of the family of the Furnivals? [Ha ! Ha ! ha !]

WITWOUD.

Aye, aye, but that was for a while, not long, not long. Pshaw ! I was not in my own power then; an orphan, and this fellow was my guardian. Aye, aye, I was glad to consent to that man to come to London. He had the disposal of me then. If I had

469 prentice: apprentice

469–70 felt-maker: maker of cloth by rolling and pressing wool

478 the wind serve: the wind give assistance

480 weathercock: revolving pointer in the shape of a cock mounted on a high place to show which way the wind blows. Hence, an inconstant person

483 the peace: Sir Wilful hopes that the Peace of Ryswick (1697), which had stopped the war with France, would continue. This would decrease the taxes on land, increase his income and enable him 'to see foreign parts'. The Peace, however, was broken in 1701, one year after this play was acted.

485 at all adventures: come what may

487 dainty: fastidious

488 shill I, shall I: indecisive, shilly-shally

490 lingo: speech or vocabulary of a special class of people

491 a spice: a bit

not agreed to that, I might have been bound prentice to a felt-maker in Shrewsbury; this fellow would have bound me to a maker of felts.

SIR WILFULL.

'Sheart, and better than to be bound to a maker of fops, where, I suppose, you have served your time; and now you may set up for yourself.

MRS. MARWOOD.

You intend to travel, sir, as I'm informed.

SIR WILFULL.

Belike I may, madam. I may chance to sail upon the salt seas, if my mind hold.

PETULANT.

And the wind serve.

SIR WILFULL.

Serve or not serve, I shan't ask licence of you, sir; nor the weathercock your companion. I direct my discourse to the lady, sir. 'Tis like my aunt may have told you, madam. Yes, I have settled my concerns, I may say now, and am minded to see foreign parts. If an how that the peace holds, whereby, that is, taxes abate.

MRS. MARWOOD.

I thought you had designed for France at all adventures.

SIR WILFULL.

I can't tell that; 'tis like I may, and 'tis like I may not. I am somewhat dainty in making a resolution, because when I make it, I keep it. I don't stand shill I, shall I, then; if I say't, I'll do't. But I have thoughts to tarry a small matter in town, to learn somewhat of your lingo first, before I cross the seas. I'd gladly have a spice of your French, as they say, whereby to hold discourse in foreign countries.

MRS. MARWOOD.

Here is an academy in town for that use.

494 'Tis like there may: most probably
496 like a … whale-fishing: Witwoud is sarcastic since the Dutch were known for their supposed robustness and boorishness
510 rallier: one who indulges in rallying, ie, raillery
511 rally … to choose: make fun of their best friends by choice

SIR WILFULL.

There is? 'Tis like there may.

MRS. MARWOOD.

No doubt you will return very much improved.

WITWOUD.

Yes, refined, like a Dutch skipper from a whale-fishing.

Enter Lady Wishfort *and* Fainall.

LADY WISHFORT.

Nephew, your are welcome.

SIR WILFULL.

Aunt, your servant.

FAINALL.

Sir Wilfull, your most faithful servant.

SIR WILFULL.

Cousin Fainall, give me your hand.

LADY WISHFORT.

Cousin Witwoud, your servant; Mr. Petulant, your servant. Nephew, you are welcome again. Will you drink anything after your journey, nephew, before you eat? Dinner's almost ready.

SIR WILFULL.

I'm very well, I thank you, aunt; however, I thank you for your courteous offer. 'Sheart, I was afraid you would have been in the fashion too, and have remembered to have forgot your relations. Here's your cousin Tony; belike I mayn't call him brother for fear of offence.

LADY WISHFORT.

Oh, he's a rallier, nephew. My cousin's a wit; and your great wits always rally their best friends to choose. When you have been abroad, nephew, you'll understand raillery better.

Fainall *and* Mrs. Marwood *talk apart.*

515 dinner is impatient: an instance of Mincing's absurd mimicry of affected speech
519 Fie: expression of outraged propriety
524 rank: offensive, loathsome
527 anticipated cuckold: one who is to be cuckolded in future (cp 'cuckold in embryo')
528 budding: growing
antlers: branched horns of deer
528 satyr: a Greek or Roman woodland deity having human form with goat's ears, tails, legs and horns
528–29 citizen's child: citizens and merchants were conventionally made fun of as cuckolds
532 outstripped: outpaced
532 scurvy wedlock: disgraceful marriage

SIR WILFULL.

Why then, let him hold his tongue in the meantime, and rail when that day comes.

Enter Mincing.

MINCING.

Mem, I come to acquaint your la'ship that dinner is impatient.

SIR WILFULL.

Impatient? Why then, belike it won't stay till I pull off my boots. Sweetheart, can you help me to a pair of slippers? My man's with his horses, I warrant.

LADY WISHFORT.

Fie, fie nephew, you would not pull off your boots here. Go down into the hall; dinner shall stay for you. My nephew's a little unbred; you'll pardon him, madam. Gentlemen, will you walk? Marwood?

MRS. MARWOOD.

I'll follow you, madam, before Sir Wilfull is ready.

Exeunt all but Mrs. Marwood *and* Fainall.

FAINALL.

Why then, Foible's a bawd, an arrant, rank, match-making bawd. And I, it seems, am a husband, a rank husband and my wife a very arrant, rank wife, all in the way of the world. 'Sdeath, to be an anticipated cuckold, a cuckold in embryo ! Sure I was born with budding antlers, like a young satyr, or a citizen's child. 'Sdeath, to be outwitted, to be out-jilted, out-matrimonied! If I had kept my speed like a stag, 'twere somewhat; but to crawl after, with my horns like a snail, and outstripped by my wife, 'tis scurvy wedlock.

MRS. MARWOOD.

Then shake if off. You have often wished for an opportunity to part; and now you have it. But first prevent their plot; the half of Millamant's fortune is too considerable to be parted with, to a foe, to Mirabell.

537–38 fond discovery: foolish revelation

539 lustre: shine

541 deputy-lieutenant's hall: the hall of a deputy-lieutenant, an important person, was often decorated with many antlers on the walls

542 cap of maintenance: 'a kind of cap, with two points like horns behind, borne in the arms of certain families' (OED). Horns suggest cuckolding which will help to maintain Fainall financially

543 away with your wife: manage to continue your present relationship with your wife

544 game: refers to Mrs Fainall's love-affair with Mirabell

547 Pam: jack of clubs, highest card in the game of loo. The cunning Fainall suspects that his wife may have given up Mirabell, but has something up her sleeve

548 to keep you: to maintain financially

553 composition: compromise

557 conjuncture: combination of events

557 warm: enraged, excited

559 appearance: Fainall says that the strategy is convincing

FAINALL.

Damn him ! that had been mine, had you not made that fond discovery. That had been forfeited, had they been married. My wife had added lustre to my horns by that increase of fortune; I could have worn'em tipt with gold, though my forehead had been furnished like a deputy lieutenant's hall.

MRS. MARWOOD.

They may prove a cap of maintenance to you still, if you can away with your wife. And she's no worse than when you had her. I dare swear she had given up her game before she was married.

FAINALL.

Hum! That may be. She might throw up her cards; but I'll be hanged if she did not put Pam in her pocket.

MRS. MARWOOD.

You married her to keep you; and if you can contrive to have her keep you better than you expected, why should you not keep her longer than you intended?

FAINALL.

The means, the means.

MRS. MARWOOD.

Discover to my lady your wife's conduct; threaten to part with her. My lady loves her, and will come to any composition to save her reputation. Take the opportunity of breaking it, just upon the discovery of this imposture. My lady will be enraged beyond bounds, and sacrifice niece and fortune and all, at that conjuncture. And let me alone to keep her warm; if she should flag in her part, I will not fail to prompt her.

FAINALL.

Faith, this has an appearance.

MRS. MARWOOD.

I'm sorry I hinted to my lady to endeavour a match between Millamant and Sir Wilfull; that may be an obstacle.

562 disable: incapacitate
563 drink like a Dane: drink to excess (supposedly like a Dane). See *Hamlet*.
563–64 set his hand in: start him off on his drinking
566ff In Fainall's rationalisation of the institution of marriage we encounter the modish and shallow nihilism that is distinctive to upper-class Restoration culture.
567 played the jade: acted the part of a woman of dubious character
569 jealous: doubtful
570 repose: rest
577 wherewithal to stake: money to bet or wager
583 branches: if 'cuckoldom' represents the branches (where marriage is the root), then the branches may also suggest the cuckold's horns
588 incendiary: person stirring up strife

FAINALL.

Oh, for that matter leave me to manage him; I'll disable him for that. He will drink like a Dane; after dinner, I'll set his hand in.

MRS. MARWOOD.

Well, how do you stand affected towards your lady?

FAINALL.

Why, faith, I'm thinking of it. Let me see. I am married already, so that's over. My wife has played the jade with me; well, that's over too. I never loved her, or if I had, why that would have been over too by this time. Jealous of her I cannot be, for I am certain; so there's an end of jealousy. Weary of her I am, and shall be. No there's no end of that; no, no that were too much to hope. Thus far concerning my repose; now for my reputation. As to my own, I married not for it; so that's out of the question. And as to my part in my wife's, why she had parted with hers before; so bringing none to me, she can take none from me. 'Tis against all rule of play that I should lose to one who has not wherewithal to stake.

MRS. MARWOOD.

Besides, you forget, marriage is honourable.

FAINALL

Hum! Faith, and that's well thought on. Marriage is honourable, as you say; and if so, wherefore should cuckoldom be a discredit, being derived from so honourable a root?

MRS. MARWOOD.

Nay; I know not; if the root be honourable, why not the branches?

FAINALL.

So, so; why this point's clear. Well, how do we proceed?

MRS. MARWOOD.

I will contrive a letter which shall be delivered to my lady at the time when that rascal who is to act Sir Rowland is with her. It shall come as from an unknown hand, for the less I appear to know of the truth, the better I can play the incendiary.

590 passages: interchanges of confidences
591 mine be sprung: let the mine (hidden explosive) burst
593 turn … grass: retire from service (used for horses)
604 herd: as a metaphor not inappropriate to the imagery of horns
605 badge: distinctive mark of a coterie or community
607 crest: perhaps a pun on 1) device above shield and helmet on coat of arms and 2) comb or tuft or plume as in coxcomb (a near cousin of cuckold)
608 or pain or shame: either pain or shame

Besides, I would not have Foible provoked if I could help it, because you know she knows some passages. Nay, I expect all will come out; but let the mine be sprung first, and then I care not if I'm discovered.

FAINALL.

If the worst come to the worst, I'll turn my wife to grass. I have already a deed of settlement of the best part of her estate, which I have wheedled out of her; and that you shall partake at least.

MRS. MARWOOD.

I hope you are convinced that I hate Mirabell; now you'll be no more jealous.

FAINALL.

Jealous ! No, by this kiss. Let husbands be jealous; but let the lover still believe. Or if he doubt, let it be only to endear his pleasure, and prepare the joy that follows, when he proves his mistress true. But let husbands' doubts convert to endless jealousy; or if they have belief, let it corrupt to superstition and blind credulity. I am single, and will herd no more with 'em. True, I wear the badge, but I'll disown the order. And since I take my leave of 'em, I care not if I leave 'em a common motto to their common crest:

All husbands must or pain or shame endure;
The wise too jealous are, fools too secure. *Exeunt.*

[IV]

3ff The elaborate preparations for Sir Rowland amount to a delightful travesty of courtly decorum since he is a fake

3 sconces: candlesticks with handles or brackets to fix on walls

4 footmen: liveried servants attending at door or table or in carriage

5 postilion: servant riding the near horse of the front horses of a carriage fill ...equipage: arrange the display to perfection

6 pulvilled: dusted with fragrant powder

14ff In Lady Wishfort's anxiety about the manner in which she should receive Sir Rowland we encounter the Restoration and Augustan view of life as performance, as masquerade; all aspects of human behaviour are thereby 'purged' of spontaneity

21 loll: sit or stand in a lazy attitude

22 jogging: shaking

Act IV, Scene I

Scene continues.
Enter Lady Wishfort *and* Foible.

LADY WISHFORT.
Is Sir Rowland coming, say'st thou, Foible? and are things in order?

FOIBLE.
Yes, madam, I have put wax lights in the sconces, and placed the footmen in a row in the hall, in their best liveries, with the coachman and postilion to fill up the equipage.

LADY WISHFORT.
Have you pulvilled the coachman and postilion that they may not stink of the stable when Sir Rowland comes by?

FOIBLE.
Yes, madam.

LADY WISHFORT.
And are the dancers and the music ready, that he may be entertained in all points with correspondence to his passion?

FOIBLE.
All is ready, madam.

LADY WISHFORT.
And—well—and how do I look Foible?

FOIBLE.
Most killing well, madam.

LADY WISHFORT.
Well, and how shall I receive him? In what figure shall I give his heart the first impression? There is a great deal in the first impression. Shall I sit?—No, I won't sit—I'll walk—aye, I'll walk from the door upon his entrance; and then turn full upon him.—No, that will be too sudden. I'll lie—aye, I'll lie down—I'll receive him in my little dressing room; there's a couch—yes, yes, I'll give the first impression on a couch.— I won't lie neither, but loll and lean upon one elbow, with one foot a little dangling off, jogging in a thoughtful way—yes—

23 start: change position abruptly, as in surprise

25 levée: the action of rising from a bed or couch, usually associated with royalty; Lady Wishfort affects French sophistication and royal status.

27 recomposing airs: the manner of settling down after agitation

32 is set in to: has begun in full swing

33 Ods my life: *God save: my life*

41ff In Millamant's pensive, absent mood and recollection of poetry we have a rare glimpse in Restoration Comedy into the inner world of a character in love Note how adroitly Congreve avoids the pitfall of sentimentalism by comically juxtaposing the uncomprehending, uncomfortable Sir Wilfull reluctantly thrust into the role of a suitor

43–44 The opening lines of an untitled poem by Sir John Suckling (1609–42), a Cavalier poet

and then as soon as he appears, start, aye, start and be surprised, and rise to meet him in a pretty disorder—yes—oh, nothing is more alluring than a levée from a couch in some confusion. —It shows the foot to advantage, and furnishes with blushes, and recomposing airs beyond comparison. Hark ! There's a coach.

FOIBLE.

'Tis he, madam.

LADY WISHFORT.

Oh dear, has my nephew made his addresses to Millamant? I ordered him.

FOIBLE

Sir Wilfull is set in to drinking, madam, in the parlour.

LADY WISHFORT.

Ods my life, I'll send him to her. Call her down, Foible; bring her hither. I'll send him as I go. When they are together, then come to me Foible, that I may not be too long alone with Sir Rowland. *Exit.*

Enter Mrs. Millamant *and* Mrs. Fainall.

FOIBLE

Madam, I stayed here, to tell your ladyship that Mr. Mirabell has waited this half hour for an opportunity to talk with you, though my lady's orders were to leave you and Sir Wilfull together. Shall I tell Mr. Mirabell that you are at leisure?

MILLAMANT.

No—what would the dear man have? I am thoughtful and would amuse myself—bid him come another time.
There never yet was woman made,
Not shall, but to be cursed. [*Repeating and walking about.*]
That's hard!

MRS. FAINALL.

You are very fond of Sir John Suckling today, Millamant, and the poets.

47 filthy verses: Cavalier poetry was often marked by licentiousness. This touch of bawdiness lends authenticity to Millamant's passion for Mirabell.

52 The opening line of *The Story of Phoebus and Daphne, Applied* by Edmund Waller (1606–87), one of the leaders of the movement away from the school of Donne towards stylistic smoothness and metrical regularity.

53–54 philosophy to undergo: resignation (perhaps stoic) to suffer

56 proxy: substitute

MILLAMANT.

He? Aye, and filthy verses; so I am.

FOIBLE.

Sir Wilfull is coming, madam. Shall I send Mr. Mirabell away?

MILLAMANT.

Aye, if you please, Foible, send him away—or send him hither—just as you will, dear Foible.—I think I'll see him—shall I? Aye, let the wretch come. *Exit Foible*

Thyrsis, a youth of the inspired train. [*Repeating.*]

Dear Fainall, entertain Sir Wilfull. Thou hast philosophy to undergo a fool; thou art married and hast patience. I would confer with my own thoughts.

MRS. FAINALL.

I am obliged to you, that you would make me your proxy in this affair; but I have business of my own.

Enter Sir Wilfull.

O Sir Wilfull, you are come at the critical instant. There's your mistress up to the ears in love and contemplation; pursue your point, now or never.

SIR WILFULL.

Yes; my aunt would have it so. I would gladly have been encourged with a bottle or two, because I'm somewhat wary at first, before I am acquainted. [*This while* Millamant *walks about repeating to herself.*] But I hope, after a time, I shall break my mind; that is, upon further acquaintance. So for the present, cousin, I'll take my leave. If so be you'll be so kind to make my excuse, I'll return to my company.

MRS. FAINALL.

Oh, fie Sir Wilfull ! What, you must not be daunted.

SIR WILFULL.

Daunted ! No, that's not it. It is not so much for that; for if so be that I set on't, I'll do't. But only for the present; 'tis sufficient till further acquaintance, that's all. Your servant.

76 'aa: she

77 vixen: characteristic of a she-fox, ie, of a quarrelsome woman

80–81 These two lines and the three which Millamant next repeats constitute the first stanza of an untitled poem by Suckling

82 Anan?: *What?*

88 easy Suckling: This description of Suckling's style once again highlights smoothness and regularity

89ff The conversation at cross-purposes between Millamant and Sir Wilfull exposes the limitations of both town and country: the rusticity of the latter cannot match the literary refinement of the former but its plain speech is preferable to polite conversation. Millamant's whimsicality, here as elsewhere, is an index to the unsettling force of the passions.

89 Suckling: Sir Wilfull thinks that Millamant is calling him utterly inexperienced (suckling = unweaned child of an animal)

90 stripling: young boy

91 ruder than Gothic: more uncivilised than a barbarian

MRS. FAINALL.

Nay, I'll swear you shall never lose so favourable an opportunity, if I can help it. I'll leave you together and lock the door. *Exit.*

SIR WILFULL.

Nay, nay cousin. I have forgot my gloves. What d'ye do? 'Sheart, 'aa has locked the door indeed, I think. Nay, Cousin Fainall, open the door ! Pshaw, what a vixen trick is this? Nay, now 'aa has seen me too. Cousin, I made bold to pass through as it were. I think this door's enchanted !

MILLAMANT [*repeating*]

I prithee spare me, gentle boy,
Press me no more for that slight toy—

SIR WILFULL.

Anan? Cousin, your servant.

MILLAMANT [*repeating*].

That foolish trifle of a heart—
Sir Wilfull !

SIR WILFULL.

Yes. Your servant. No offence, I hope, cousin.

MILLAMANT [*repeating*].

I swear it will not do its part,
Though thou dost thine, employ'st thy power and art.
Natural, easy Suckling !

SIR WILFULL.

Anan? Suckling? No such suckling neither, cousin, nor stripling; I thank heaven, I'm no minor.

MILLAMANT.

Ah, rustic ! ruder than Gothic!

SIR WILFLL.

Well, well. I shall understand your lingo one of these days, cousin; in the meanwhile, I must answer in plain English.

96 to fetch a walk: to go for a walk

98 fought: fetched, as above

106 Ah, *l'étourdie*: The expression could refer to dizzying urban life or to Sir Wilfull as a fool, since it could mean 'giddy' or 'scatter-brained'.

MILLAMANT.

Have you any business with me, Sir Wilfull?

SIR WILFULL.

Not at present, cousin. Yes, I made bold to see, to come and know it that how you were disposed to fetch a walk this evening, if so be that I might not be troublesome, I would have fought a walk with you.

MILLAMANT.

A walk! What then?

SIR WILFULL.

Nay, nothing. Only for the walk's sake, that's all.

MILLAMANT.

I nauseate walking; 'tis a country diversion. I loathe the country and everything that relates to it.

SIR WILFULL.

Indeed! Ha! Look ye, look ye, you do? Nay, 'tis like you may. Here are choice of pastimes here in town, as plays and the like; that must be confessed indeed.

MILIMANT.

Ah, *l'étourdie !* I hate the town too.

SIR WILFULL.

Dear heart, that's much. Ha! that you should hate 'em both! Ha! 'tis like you may; there are some can't relish the town, and others can't away with the country. 'Tis like you may be one of those, cousin.

MILLAMANT.

Ha! ha! ha! Yes, 'tis like I may. You havc nothing further to say to me?

SIR WILFULL.

Not at present, cousin. 'Tis like when I have an opportunity to be more private, I may break my mind in some measure. I conjecture you partly guess.—However, that's as time shall try; but spare to speak and spare to speed, as they say.

119 all a case: it doesn't matter

129 The third line of the poem by Waller quoted above by Millamant. Mirabell, entering, completes the couplet indicating affinity in breeding and background.

130ff With the entry of Mirabell begins the sustained wit-combat of the proviso scene. The wit carries within it a subtext of emotion or rather, wit becomes the specific vehicle of emotion The *joie de vivre* and vitality that bubble up through the elegant language transform it from an instrument of manipulative *politesse* to one suggesting the uncalculating enjoyment by the lovers of each other's company Even as Millamant desires a measure of freedom in married life, a room of one's own, the lovers engage (somewhat like Benedick and Beatrice in *Much Ado About Nothing*) in a critique of the false and meagre conventions of love and marriage.

131 curious: minutely careful
artifice: trick

136 solicit me: court me

136 grate: grating, door with parallel or crossed metal bars

MILLAMANT.

If it is of no great importance, Sir Wilfull, you will oblige me to leave me; I have just now a little business—

SIR WILFULL.

Enough, enough, cousin, yes, yes, all a case; when you're disposed, when you're disposed. Now's as well as another time; and another time as well as now. All's one for that. Yes, yes, if your concerns call you, there's no haste; it will keep cold, as they say. Cousin, your servant. I think this door's locked.

MILLAMANT.

You may go this way, sir.

SIR WILFULL.

Your servant; then with your leave I'll return to my company. *Exit.*

MILLAMANT.

Aye, aye; ha! ha! ha!
Like Phoebus sung the no less amorous boy.

Enter Mirabell.

MIRABELL.

Like Daphne she, as lovely and as coy.
Do you lock yourself up from me, to make my search more curious? Or is this pretty artifice contrived, to signify that here the chase must end and my pursuit be crowned, for you can fly no further?

MILLAMANT.

Vanity ! No. I'll fly and be followed to the last moment. Though I am upon the very verge of matrimony, I expect you should solicit me as much as if I were wavering at the grate of monastery, with one foot over the threshold. I'll be solicited to the very last, nay and afterwards.

MIRABELL.

What, after the last?

MILLAMANT.

Oh, I should think I was poor and had nothing to bestow, if I

151 pedantic: dogmatic
152 pragmatical: self-assured
156 grace: ie, the prayer concluding the wedding ceremony
160 *douceurs*: sweetnesses, pleasures
160 *sommeils du matin*: idle day-dreaming

were reduced to an inglorious ease and freed from the agreeable fatigues of solicitation.

MIRABELL.

But do not you know that when favours are conferred upon instant and tedious solicitation, that they diminish in their value, and that both the giver loses the grace, and the receiver lessens his pleasure?

MILLAMANT.

It may be in things of common application; but never sure in love. Oh, I hate a lover that can dare to think he draws a moment's air independent on the bounty of his mistress. There is not so impudent a thing in nature as the saucy look of an assured man, confident of success. The pedantic arrogance of a very husband has not so pragmatical an air. Ah! I'll never marry, unless I am first made sure of my will and pleasure.

MIRABELL.

Would you have 'em both before marriage? Or will you be contented with the first now, and stay for the other till after grace?

MILLAMANT.

Ah ! don't be impertinent.—My dear liberty, shall I leave thee? My faithful solitude, my darling contemplation, must I bid you then adieu? Ay-h adieu—my morning thoughts, agreeable wakings, indolent slumbers, all ye *douceurs,* ye *sommeils du matin,* adieu?—I can't do't, 'tis more than impossible. Positively, Mirabell, I'll lie abed in a morning as long as I please.

MIRABELL.

Then I'll get up in a morning as early as I please.

MILLAMANT.

Ah ! Idle creature, get up when you will.—And d'ye hear, I won't be called names after I'm married; positively I won't be called names.

170 nauseous: the comic exaggeration of this term clearly indicates the tone of the entire scene

cant: fashionable jargon peculiar to a class of people

171 fulsomely familiar: intimate in a disgustingly excessive manner. The hypocritical institution of marriage in upper-class Restoration society is under attack here

173 Fadler: one who is given to fondling

173 Hyde Park: a London park – fashionable resort in the seventeenth century; later the scene of political speeches and demonstrations

174–75 eyes and whispers: gossip

178 strange: as though estranged

185 interrogatories: questions

wry: distorted (expressing disgust)

191 inviolate: undisturbed

195 articles subscribed: clauses in an agreement guaranteed and signed

196 dwindle: shrink, decline (that is, get reconciled to by use)

MIRABELL.

Names!

MILLAMANT.

Aye, as wife, spouse, my dear, joy, jewel, love, sweetheart, and the rest of that nauseous cant, in which men and their wives are so fulsomely familiar—I shall never bear that.—Good Mirabell, don't let us be familiar or fond, nor kiss before folks, like my Lady Fadler and Sir Francis; nor go to Hyde Park together the first Sunday in a new chariot, to provoke eyes and whispers; and then never to be seen there together again; as if we were proud of one another the first week, and ashamed of one another ever after. Let us never visit together, nor go to a play together. But let us be very strange and well-bred; let us be as strange as if we had been married a great while, and as well-bred as if we were not married at all.

MIRABELL.

Have you any more conditions to offer? Hitherto your demands are pretty reasonable.

MILLAMANT.

Trifles!—As liberty to pay and receive visits to and from whom I please; to write and receive letters, without interrogatories or wry faces on your part; to wear what I please; and choose conversation with regard only to my own taste; to have no obligation upon me to converse with wits that I don't like, because they are your acquaintance; or to be intimate with fools, because they may be your relations. Come to dinner when I please; dine in my dressing room when I'm out of humour without giving a reason. To have my closet inviolate; to be sole empress of my tea table, which you must never presume to approach without first asking leave. And lastly, wherever I am, you shall always knock at the door before you come in. These articles subscribed, if I continue to endure you a little longer, I may by degrees dwindle into a wife.

197 bill of fare: menu, programme
202 *Imprimis*: in the first place (a term used in legal contracts)
202 covenant: lay down as in a contract
203 confidante: female companion trusted with secrets, especially of love. Mirabell is contemptuous of the secret intrigues conducted by women under cover of intimacy
206 no decoy-duck … mask: no 'female confidante who will persuade a fop to rush you, masked, to the theatre'
212 article: lay down
214 new-coin it: produce a new face with the use of make-up
215 vizards: visors or masks
216 Hog's bones … roasted cat: supposed to be ingredients in cosmetics
218 commerce …Court: transaction or dealing with a peddler of cosmetics
220 atlases: 'silk-satin manufactured in the East' (OED)
breeding: pregnant

MIRABELL.

Your bill of fare is something advanced in this latter account. Well, have I liberty to offer conditions—that when you are dwindled into a wife, I may not be beyond measure enlarged into a husband?

MILLAMANT.

You have free leave. Propose your utmost; speak and spare not.

MIRABELL.

I thank you. *Imprimis* then, I covenant that your acquaintance be general; that you admit no sworn confidante, or intimate of your own sex; no she-friend to screen her affairs under your countenance, and tempt you to make trial of a mutual secrecy. No decoy-duck to wheedle you a fop, scrambling to the play in a mask; then bring you home in a pretended fright, when you think you shall be found out, and rail at me for missing the play, and disappointing the frolic which you had, to pick me up and prove my constancy.

MILLAMANT.

Detestable *imprimis !* I go to the play in a mask !

MIRABELL.

Item, I article that you continue to like your own face as long as I shall; and while it passes current with me, that you endeavour not to new-coin it. To which end, together with all vizards for the day, I prohibit all masks for the night, made of oiled skins and I know now what—hog's bones, hare's gall, pig-water, and the marrow of a roasted cat. In short, I forbid all commerce with the gentlewoman in What-d'ye-call-it Court. *Item,* I shunt my doors against all bawds with baskets, and pennyworths of muslin, china, fans, atlases, etc.—*Item,* when you shall be breeding—

MILLAMANT.

Ah ! name it not.

MIRABELL.

Which may be presumed, with a blessing on our endeavours—

225 strait-lacing: tightly-laced corsets used to squeeze a woman's body into a slender shape

226 sugar-loaf: conical moulded mass of sugar. The term is used sometimes to describe a conical hill

227 billet: small stick or bar of metal

236 auxiliaries: allied or foreign troops

236 orange brandy … clary: varieties of flavoured brandy
aniseed: seed of anise used as a carminative
cinnamon: aromatic inner bark of East Indies tree used as spice
citron: lemon-like fruit or its tree

238 cowslip-wine: wine made from wild plant growing in pastures, with fragrant yellow flowers. Mirabell allows this drink presumably because of its low alcohol content.

239 dormitives: sleep-inducing drinks

240 tractable: manageable, docile

MILLAMANT.

Odious endeavours!

MIRABELL.

I denounce against all strait-lacing, squeezing for a shape, till you mould my boy's head like a sugar-loaf, and instead of a man-child, make me the father to a crooked billet. Lastly, to the dominion of the tea table I submit, but with proviso, that you exceed not in your province, but restrain yourself to native and simple tea-table drinks, as tea, chocolate, and coffee. As likewise to genuine and authorised tea-table talk—such as mending of fashions, spoiling reputations, railing at absent friends, and so forth; but that on no account you encroach upon the men's prerogative, and presume to drink healths, or toast fellows; for prevention of which, I banish all foreign forces, all auxiliaries to the tea table, as orange brandy, all aniseed, cinnamon, citron, and Barbadoes waters, together with ratafia and the most noble spirit of clary. But for cowslip-wine, poppy-water, and all dormitives, those I allow. These provisos admitted, in other things I may prove a tractable and complying husband.

MILLAMANT.

Oh, horrid provisos ! filthy strong waters ! I toast fellows, odious men ! I hate your odious provisos.

MIRABELL.

Then we're agreed. Shall I kiss your hand upon the contract? And here comes one to be a witness to the sealing of the deed.

Enter Mrs. Fainall.

MILLAMANT.

Fainall, what shall I do? Shall I have him? I think I must have him.

MRS. FAINALL.

Aye, aye, take him, take him, what should you do?

MILLAMANT.

Well then—I'll take my death I'm in a horrid fright—Fainall, I shall never say it—well—I think—I'll endure you.

258 a necessity for your obedience: Mirabell is not even given the time to utter a word in response. An emotionally charged moment is juxtaposed with the urgency of intrigue where there is little scope for emotion. The comedy of sexual love blends with the comedy of trickery.

275 Millamant's abstracted mood in love is turned to delicate comedy once again by the context of practical difficulties.

MRS. FAINALL.

Fie, fie ! have him, have him, and tell him so in plain terms; for I am sure you have a mind to him.

MILLAMANT.

Are you? I think I have—and the horrid man looks as if he thought so too.—Well, you ridiculous thing you, I'll have you—I won't be kissed, nor I won't be thanked—here, kiss my hand though. —So, hold your tongue now, and don't say a word.

MRS. FAINALL.

Mirabell, there's a necessity for your obedience; you have neither time to talk nor stay. My mother is coming; and in my conscience, if she should see you, would fall into fits and maybe not recover, time enough to return to Sir Rowland, who as Foible tells me, is in fair way to succeed. Therefore spare your ecstasies for another occasion, and slip down the backstairs, where Foible waits to consult you.

MILLAMANT.

Aye, go, go. In the meantime I suppose you have said something to please me.

MIRABELL.

I am all obedience. *Exit.*

MRS. FAINALL.

Yonder Sir Wilfull's drunk, and so noisy that my mother has been forced to leave Sir Rowland to appease him; but he answers her only with singing and drinking. What they have done by this time I know not; but Petulant and he were quarrelling as I came by.

MILLAMANT.

Well, if Mirabell should not make a good husband, I am a lost thing—for I find I love him violently.

MRS. FAINALL.

So it seems, when you mind not what's said to you. If you doubt him, you had best take up with Sir Wilfull.

278 fray: quarrel
279ff Sir Wilfull's drunkenness and the 'quarrel' with Petulant bring in a note of Rabelaisian disorder into the tinsel world of elegance.
280 christenings: baptisms
281 pieced: enlarged with additional pieces
camlet: expensive Eastern fabric
283 *nolle prosequi*: (legal) relinquishment by plaintiff or prosecutor of his suit
287 a sputtering: emitting spitting, crackling sound
290 whim it about: spin
292 nymph: Petulant tries to use the stilted conventions of pastoral romance or eclogue.
294 folios: sheets of paper folded once and made into a book
decimo sexto: sheet of paper folded in sixteen leaves; book made out of these
295 Lacedemonian: Spartans were renowned for being laconic
295 epitomiser: one who summarises

MILLAMANT.

How can you name that superannuated lubber? foh !

Enter Witwoud *from drinking.*

MRS. FAINALL.

So, is the fray made up, that you have left 'em?

WITWOUD.

Left 'em? I could stay no longer. I have laughed like ten christenings; I am tipsy with laughing. If I had stayed any longer I should have burst; I must have been let out and pieced in the sides like an unsized camlet. Yes, yes, the fray is composed; my lady came in like a *nolle prosequi* and stopped their proceedings.

MILLAMANT.

What was the dispute?

WITWOUD.

That's the jest; there was no dispute. They could neither of 'em speak for rage, and so fell a sputtering at one another like two roasting apples.

Enter Petulant *drunk.*

Now Petulant, all's over, all's well. Gad, my head begins to whim it about. Why dost thou not speak? Thou art both as drunk and as mute as a fish.

PETULANT.

Look you, Mrs. Millamant, if you can love me, dear nymph, say it, and that's the conclusion. Pass on, or pass off; that's all.

WITWOUD.

Thou hast uttered volumes, folios, in less than *decimo sexto*, my dear Lacedemonian. Sirrah Petulant, thou art an epitomiser of words.

PETULANT.

Witwoud, you are an annihilator of sense.

299 pincushions: small cushions for sticking in pins ready for use, often made with shreds and bits

301 Baldwin: the ass in the story of Reynard the fox

gemini: twins

304 bite: Witwoud admires the supposedly biting wit of Petulant

mustard seed: pungent paste made from mustard seeds

307 like a radish: ie, causing the discomfort of flatulence

310 enow: enough

312 castanets: hardwood or ivory instruments used in pairs to rattle in time with dancing

316 conclude premises: bring matters to a conclusion

320 wrap … wood louse: refers to the insect's ability to roll itself up in a ball

WITWOUD.

Thou art a retailer of phrases and dost deal in remnants of remnants, like a maker of pincushions; thou art in truth (metaphorically speaking) a speaker of shorthand.

PETULANT.

Thou art (without a figure) just one half of an ass, and Baldwin yonder, thy half brother, is the rest. A gemini of asses split would make just four of you.

WITWOUD.

Thou dost bite, my dear mustard seed; kiss me for that.

PETULANT.

Stand off! I'll kiss no more males. I have kissed your twin yonder in a humour of reconciliation, till he [*hiccup*] rises upon my stomach like a radish.

MILLAMANT.

Eh! filthy creature! What was the quarrel?

PETULANT.

There was no quarrel; there might have been a quarrel.

WITWOUD.

If there had been words enow between 'em to have expressed provocation, they had gone together by the ears like a pair of castanets.

PETULANT.

You were the quarrel.

MILLAMANT.

Me!

PETULANT.

If I have a humour to quarrel, I can make less matters conclude premises. If you are not handsome, what then, if I have a humour to prove it? If I shall have my reward, say so; if not, fight for your face the next time yourself. I'll go sleep.

WITWOUD.

Do, wrap thyself up like wood louse, and dream revenge; and

323 Carry …spider: possibly a bawdy reference
flea: pick fleas
325 pickle: mess
328 comport: behave, conduct
329 rantipole: ill-mannered
333 borachio: drunkard. Borachio is the name of a minor character in *Much Ado About Nothing.*
336 best foot foremost: go at full pace
337 grutch: grudge
341 potent and mellow: strong and matured

hear me, if thou canst learn to write by tomorrow morning, pen me a challenge. I'll carry it for thee.

PETULANT.

Carry your mistress' monkey a spider ! Go flea dogs, and read romances! I'll go to bed to my maid. *Exit.*

MRS. FAINALL.

He's horridly drunk. How came you all in this pickle?

WITWOUD.

A plot ! a plot ! to get rid of the knight. Your husband's advice; but he sneaked off.

Enter Lady Wishfort, *and* Sir Wilfull *drunk.*

LADY WISHFORT.

Out upon't, out upon't! At years of discretion, and comport yourself at this rantipole rate !

SIR WILFULL.

No offence, aunt.

LADY WISHFORT.

Offence? As I'm a person, I'm ashamed of you—foh ! how you stink of wine ! D'ye think my niece will ever endure such a borachio! you're an absolute borachio.

SIR WILFULL.

Borachio !

LADY WISHFORT.

At a time when you should commence an amour and put your best foot foremost—

SIR WILFULL.

'Sheart, an you grutch me your liquor, make a bill. Give me more drink, and take my purse. *Sings.*

Prithee fill me the glass,
Till it laugh in my face,
With ale that is potent and mellow;
He that whines for a lass
Is an ignorant ass,

344 bumper: full glass of wine
348 overtaken: overwhelmed
350 *In vino veritas*: in wine there is truth, ie, people speak the truth when they are drunk
354 spits: A reference perhaps to vomiting or to Witwoud's inability to hold his liquor.
362 pimple: jolly companion
soaker: hard drinker
cellar: place (often underground) for storing wine
363 Antipodes: the region directly opposite to us on the globe
364 topsy-turvy fellows: because (being in the Antipodes) they live upside down
367-69 Bawdy references to loss of virginity and pregnancy.
373 a tallow chandler: a maker or seller of candles made of tallow, ie, animal fat. Chandlers were thus thought to have a strong, foul smell.

For a bumper has not its fellow.

But if you would have me marry my cousin, say the word, and I'll do't. Wilfull will do't; that's the word. Wilfull will do't; that's my crest. My motto I have forgot.

LADY WISHFORT.

My nephew's a little overtaken, cousin, but 'tis with drinking your health. O' my word you are obliged to him.

SIR WILFULL.

In vino veritas, aunt. If I drunk your health today, cousin, I am a borachio. But if you have a mind to be married, say the word, and send for the piper; Wilfull will do't. If not, dust it away, and let's have t'other round.—Tony !—Ods-heart, where's Tony?—Tony's an honest fellow; but he spits after a bumper, and that's a fault.

We'll drink, and we'll never ha' done, boys, *Sings.*
  Put the glass then around with the sun, boys;
Let Apollo's example invite us;
  For he's drunk every night,
  And that makes him so bright,
  That he's able next morning to light us.

The sun's good pimple, an honest soaker; he has a cellar at your Antipodes. If I travel, aunt, I touch at your Antipodes; your Antipodes are a good, rascally sort of topsy-turvy fellows. If I had a bumper, I'd stand upon my head and drink a health to 'em. A match, or no match, cousin with the hard name? Aunt, Wilfull will do't. If she has her maidenhead, let her look to't; if she has not, let her keep her own counsel in the meantime, and cry out at the nine months' end.

MILLAMANT.

Your pardon, madam, I can stay no longer. Sir Wilfull grows very powerful. Egh ! how he smells ! I shall be overcome if I stay. Come, cousin.

Exeunt Millamant *and* Mrs. Fainall.

LADY WISHFORT.

Smells ! he would poison a tallow chandler and his family. Beastly creature, I know not what to do with him ! Travel,

375 quotha: indeed ('says he')
376 Saracens: nomadic people of Syro-Arabian desert; Arabs or Moslems of the time of the Crusades
Tartars: a Central Asian race
378 pagan: ie, not enlightened like the Christians
379 infidels: disbelievers in the true religion
380 grape: ie, drinking, as well as emblem of Christ's body crushed to produce wine (blood transubstantiated)
380–81 dry stinkard: stinking teetotaller
383 Mufti: Mohammedan priest or expounder of law
384 claret: French red wine, usually from Bordeaux
388 heathenish: unenlightened (originally, non-Christian, non-Jewish, non-Moslem)
392 sophy: the Shah of Persia
395 tumbril: heavy cart
sot: stupefied by drinking
396 bastinadoed: beaten on the soles of the feet
400 moment: importance
400–01 invades … precipitation: assails me with the utmost urgency
404 cock-match: cock-fight. Wilfull finds an obscene innuendo in it.

quotha ! aye, travel, travel, get thee gone, get thee but far enough, to the Saracens, or the Tartars, or the Turks, for thou art not fit to live in a Christian commonwealth, thou beastly pagan !

SIR WILFULL.

Turks, no; no Turks, aunt; your Turks are infidels, and believe not in the grape. Your Mahometan, your Mussulman, is a dry stinkard. No offence, aunt. My map says that your Turk is not so honest a man as your Christian. I cannot find by the map that your Mufti is orthodox; whereby it is a plain case that orthodox is a hard word, aunt, and [*hiccup*] Greek for claret.

Sings.

To drink is a Christian diversion,
Unknown to the Turk and the Persian:
  Let Mahometan fools
  Live by heathenish rules,
And be damned over tea cups and coffee !
  But let British lads sing,
  Crown a health to the king,
And a fig for your sultan and sophy !
Ah, Tony !

Enter Foible, *and whispers* Lady Wishfort.

LADY WISHFORT [*aside to* Foible.]

Sir Rowland impatient? Good lack ! what shall I do with this beastly tumbril? [*Aloud.*] Go lie down and sleep, you sot! or, as I'm a person, I'll have you bastinadoed with broomsticks. Call up the wenches. *Exit* Foible.

SIR WILFULL.

Ahey ! Wenches, where are the wenches?

LADY WISHFORT.

Dear Cousin Witwoud, get him away, and you will bind me to you inviolably. I have an affair of moment that invades me with some precipitation. You will oblige me to all futurity.

WITWOUD.

Come, knight. Pox on him, I don't know what to say to him. Will you go to a cock-match?

405 shake-bag: gamecock, the largest and strongest kind of fighting-cock, able to give any opponent a good fight

405–06 bite your cheek: ie, in drunken gratitude

408 Salopian: native of Shropshire

409 Tantony: St Anthony, who conquered gluttony and was therefore pictorially represented as followed by a pig. Here on the stage, the fat Wilfull (pig) follows the thin Witwoud

414ff Simply by virtue of Waitwell's actual social status Congreve succeeds in ridiculing the stilted conventions of *politesse.* For example, the ritual of courtship (455–61) is dismantled into carnality and the sinister appetite for sex, money and power – camphor and frankincense, chastity and odour (486–87) are all covers for concupiscence An insidious relationship is thus established between the refined and the gross, whereby refinement becomes a signal for raw and ravaging lust

415 retrospection: act of looking back on the past

416 Year of Jubilee: year of remission in the Roman Catholic Church from penal consequences of sin. 1700, the year Congreve's play was first staged, was a Jubilee Year.

418 unbend the severity: relax the strictness

421–22 tantalised: tormented with hopes that do not succeed (from the fate of Tantalus punished by Zeus to stand up to the chin in water that receded whenever he stooped to drink)
tantalised on a rack: an example of mixed metaphor : Waitwell mixes up two different kinds of torture

422 tenter: tenterhook

SIR WILFULL.

With a wench, Tony? Is she a shake-bag, Sirrah? Let me bite your cheek for that.

WITWOUD.

Horrible ! He has a breath like a bagpipe ! Aye, aye, come, will you march, my Salopian?

SIR WILFULL.

Lead on, little Tony; I'll follow thee, my Anthony, my Tantony
Sirrah, thou shalt be my Tantony, and I'll be thy pig.
And a fig for your sultan and sophy.

Exit singing with Witwoud.

LADY WISHFORT.

This will never do. It will never make a match—at least before he has been abroad.

Enter Waitwell, *disguised as* Sir Rowland.

Dear Sir Rowland, I am confounded with confusion at the retrospection of my own rudeness ! I have more pardons to ask than the Pope distributes in the Year of Jubilee. But I hope, where there is likely to be so near an alliance, we may unbend the severity of decorum and dispense with a little ceremony.

WAITWELL.

My impatience, madam, is the effect of my transport; and till I have the possession of your adorable person, I am tantalised on a rack, and do but hang, madam, on the tenter of expectation.

LADY WISHFORT.

You have an excess of gallantry, Sir Rowland, and press things to a conclusion with a most prevailing vehemence. But a day or two for decency of marriage—

WAITWELL.

For decency of funeral, madam ! The delay will break my heart; or, if that should fail, I shall be poisoned. My nephew will get

429 inkling: hint, suspicion

436 respect myself: Lady Wishfort claims that her opinion is not with respect to herself

437 perfidious: treacherous

441 trances: a trance is a hypnotic state brought on by religious ecstasy

442–43 heartheavings: panting

443–44 pathetic regards: looks full of sadness and longing

451 save-all: pan with spike for burning up candle-ends. Since the candle burned right to the end, it produced a strong smell

453 labyrinth: maze

clue: clew—ball of thread or yarn used in mythological story to guide through labyrinth

455 indigestion of widowhood: inability to accept the sexual loneliness of a widow

an inkling of my designs and poison me; and I would willingly starve him before I die; I would gladly go out of the world with that satisfaction. That would be some comfort to me, if I could but live so long as to be revenged on that unnatural viper.

LADY WISHFORT.

Is he so unnatural, say you? Truly I would contribute much both to the saving of your life, and the accomplishment of your revenge. Not that I respect myself, though he has been a perfidious wretch to me.

WAITWELL.

Perfidious to you!

LADY WISHFORT.

O Sir Rowland, the hours that he has died away at my feet, the tears that he has shed, the oaths that he has sworn, the palpitations that he has felt, the trances and the tremblings, the ardours and the ecstasies, the kneelings and the risings, the heart-heavings, and the hand-grippings, the pangs and the pathetic regards of his protesting eyes! Oh, no memory can register.

WAITWELL.

What, my rival! Is the rebel my rival? 'A dies.

LADY WISHFORT.

No, don't kill him at once, Sir Rowland; starve him gradually, inch by inch.

WAITWELL.

I'll do't. In three weeks he shall be barefoot; in a month out at knees with begging an alms. He shall starve upward and upward till he has nothing living but his head, and then go out in a stink like a candle's end upon a save-all.

LADY WISHFORT.

Well, Sir Rowland, you have the way. You are no novice in the labyrinth of love; you have the clue. But as I am a person, Sir Rowland, you must not attribute my yielding to any sinister appetite, or indigestion of widowhood; nor impute my

456 lethargy of continence: slowness or slothfulness of sexual control
457 iteration of nuptials: repetition of marriage. Lady Wishfort's affected and pompous vocabulary betrays the uneasy sexual appetite of an aged woman.
460 prostitution of decorums: degradation of the rules of etiquette
466 shrine: casket or tomb or monument having holy associations
467 scruple of carnality: smallest bit of physical desire
468 camphire: camphor
frankincense: an aromatic gum resin burnt as incense

complacency to any lethargy of continence. I hope you do not think me prone to any iteration of nuptials.

WAITWELL.

Far be it from me—

LADY WISHFORT.

If you do, I protest I must recede, or think that I have made prostitution of decorums; but in the vehemence of compassion, and to save the life of a person of so much importance—

WAITWELL.

I esteem it so.

LADY WISHFORT.

Or else you wrong my condescension.

WAITWELL.

I do not, I do not!

LADY WISHFORT.

Indeed you do.

WAITWELL.

I do not, fair shrine of virtue!

LADY WISHFORT.

If you think the least scruple of carnality was an ingredient—

WAITWELL.

Dear madam, no. You are all camphire and frankincense, all chastity and odour.

LADY WISHFORT.

Or that—

Enter Foible.

FOIBLE.

Madam, the dancers are ready, and there's one with a letter, who must deliver it into your own hands.

LADY WISHFORT.

Sir Rowland, will you give me leave? Think favourably, judge candidly, and conclude you have found a person who would

476 incessantly: instantly
478 cordial: drink supposedly stimulating the heart , hence the pun on 'spirits'
479 washy: insipid, feeble
481 antidote: medicine to counteract disease or poison
484 chairman … dog-day: carrier of a sedan chair in the peak of summer
491 superscription: writing at the top of or outside something
hand: handwriting

suffer racks in honour's cause, dear Sir Rowland, and will wait on you incessantly.

Exit.

WAITWELL.

Fie, fie! What a slavery have I undergone! Spouse, hast thou any cordial? I want spirits.

FOIBLE.

What a washy rogue art thou, to pant thus for a quarter of an hour's lying and swearing to a fine lady !

WAITWELL.

Oh, she is the antidote to desire ! Spouse, thou wilt fare the worse for't. I shall have no appetite to iteration of nuptials this eight-and-forty hours. By this hand I'd rather be a chairman in the dog-day than act Sir Rowland till this time tomorrow !

Enter Lady Wishfort, *with a letter.*

LADY WISHFORT.

Call in the dancers. Sir Rowland, we'll sit, if you please, and see the entertainment.

Dance.

Now, with your permission, Sir Rowland, I will peruse my letter. I would open it in your presence, because I would not make you uneasy. If it should make you uneasy, I would burn it. Speak, if it does. But you may see by the superscription it is like a woman's hand.

FOIBLE [*aside to* Waitwell].

By heaven ! Mrs. Marwood's; I know it. My heart aches. Get it from her.

WAITWELL.

A woman's hand? No, madam, that's no woman's hand; I see that already. That's somebody whose throat must be cut.

LADY WISHFORT.

Nay, Sir Rowland, since you give me a proof of your passion by your jealousy, I promise you I'll make you a return, by a

503 abused: cheated
507 suborned: (person) bribed to tell a lie or make a false accusation
514 Roman hand: handwriting originally introduced by the Romans
520 character: style of handwriting

frank communication. You shall see it; we'll open it together. Look you here. [*Reads.*] "Madam, though unknown to you" —Look you there, 'tis from nobody that I know—"I have that honour for your character, that I think myself obliged to let you know you are abused. He who pretends to be Sir Rowland is a cheat and a rascal."—Oh, heavens ! what's this?

FOIBLE [*aside*].
Unfortunate! all's ruined!

WAITWELL.
How, how, let me see, let me see! [*Reading*] "A rascal, and disguised and suborned for that imposture."—O villainy! villainy—"by the contrivance of—"

LADY WISHFORT.
I shall faint, I shall die, I shall die, oh!

FOIBLE [*aside to* Waitwell].
Say 'tis your nephew's hand. Quickly, his plot, swear, swear it!

WAITWELL.
Here's a villain! Madam, don't you perceive it? don't you see it?

LADY WISHFORT.
Too well, too well! I have seen too much.

WAITWELL.
I told you at first I knew the hand. A woman's hand? The rascal writes a sort of a large hand, your Roman hand. I saw there was a throat to be cut presently. If he were my son, as he is my nephew, I'd pistol him!

FOIBLE.
Oh, treachery! But are you sure, Sir Rowland, it is his writing?

WAITWELL.
Sure? Am I here? Do I live? Do I love this pearl of India? I have twenty letters in my pocket from him in the same character.

LADY WISHFORT.
How!

525 stole by: went past stealthily
531 discompose: upset, disturb
533 his date is short: his days are numbered
541 conjure: appeal earnestly or solemnly

FOIBLE.

Oh, what luck it is, Sir Rowland, that you were present at this juncture! This was the business that brought Mr. Mirabell disguised to Madam Millamant this afternoon. I thought something was contriving, when he stole by me and would have hid his face.

LADY WISHFORT.

How, how! I heard the villain was in the house indeed; and now I remember, my niece went away abruptly, when Sir Wilfull was to have made his addresses.

FOIBLE.

Then, then, madam, Mr. Mirabell waited for her in her chamber, but I would not tell your ladyship to discompose you when you were to receive Sir Rowland.

WAITWELL.

Enough, his date is short.

FOIBLE.

No, good Sir Rowland, don't incur the law.

WAITWELL.

Law? I care not for law. I can but die, and 'tis in a good cause. My lady shall be satisfied of my truth and innocence, though it cost me my life.

LADY WISHFORT.

No, dear Sir Rowland, don't fight; if you should be killed, I must never show my face; or hanged—oh, consider my reputation, Sir Rowland ! No, you shan't fight. I'll go in and examine my niece; I'll make her confess. I conjure you, Sir Rowland, by all your love not to fight.

WAITWELL.

I am charmed, madam; I obey. But some proof you must let me give you; I'll go for a black box, which contains the writings of my whole estate, and deliver that into your hands.

LADY WISHFORT.

Aye, dear Sir Rowland, that will be some comfort; bring the black box.

548 A contract is indispensable to the most intimate relationship in the world of this comedy

557 an arrant knight: pun on knight-errant (wandering knight) and arrant (notorious)

WAITWELL.

And may I presume to bring a contract to be signed this night? May I hope so far?

LADY WISHFORT.

Bring what you will; but come alive, pray come alive. Oh, this is a happy discovery!

WAITWELL.

Dead or alive I'll come, and married we will be in spite of treachery; aye, and get an heir that shall defeat the last remaining glimpse of hope in my abandoned nephew. Come, my buxom widow.

Ere long you shall substantial proof receive
That I'm an arrant knight—

FOIBLE [*aside*]. Or arrant knave. *Exeunt.*

[V: In the early part of the Act, Lady Wishfort's contemptuous exposure of Foible's low origins points to an alternative urban milieu, another London of petty trade, crime and squalor sharply at odds with its polite and elegant counterpart. Restoration and especially Augustan satire characteristically straddled an ironic exchange of these two worlds, popular and polite It is thus not a coincidence that in the last part of the Act, crime and greed are exposed and punished within the polite milieu.

2 bosom traitress: woman who misuses trust and intimacy to betray

4 gauze: thin transparent fabric – silk, linen or cotton
weaving of dead hair: wig-making

5 chafing dish: vessel holding burning coal to warm dishes placed on it
starved embers: dying fire

6 traverse rag: tattered curtain

9 set up, drive: establish and carry on (a trade)

11 pack-thread: stout thread for sewing or tying up packs
bulk: store or booth

12 dead wall: suggestive of the economically depressed quarters of London
ballad-monger: selling ballads was a beggarly occupation

12 frisoneer … colberteen: cheap items of clothing

15 quilted: with padded lining
nightcap: cap worn in bed

19 governante: French for 'housekeeper'

20 feathered your nest: made yourself rich

23 dissembling: hypocritical, false

Scene continues.

Enter Lady Wishfort *and* Foible.

LADY WISHFORT.

Out of my house, out of my house, thou viper ! thou serpent, that I have fostered ! thou bosom traitress that I raised from nothing ! Begone ! begone ! begone ! go ! go ! That I took from washing of old gauze and weaving of dead hair, with a bleak blue nose, over chafing dish of starved embers, and dining behind a traverse rag, in a shop no bigger than a birdcage ! Go, go ! starve again, do, do !

FOIBLE.

Dear madam, I'll beg pardon on my knees.

LADY WISHFORT.

Away ! out ! out ! Go set up for yourself again ! Do, drive a trade, do, with your three-pennyworth of small ware, flaunting upon a pack-thread, under a brandy-seller's bulk, or against a dead wall by a ballad-monger ! Go, hang out an old frisoneer gorgette, with a yard of yellow colberteen again. Do ! an old gnawed mask, two rows of pins, and a child's fiddle; a glass necklace with the beads broken, and a quilted nightcap with one ear. Go, go, drive a trade ! These were your commodities you treacherous trull ! This was your merchandise you dealt in, when I took you into my house, placed you next to myself, and made you governante of my whole family ! You have forgot this, have you, now you have feathered your nest ?

FOIBLE.

No, no dear madam. Do but hear me; have but a moment's patience. I'll confess all. Mr. Mirabell seduced me; I am not the first that he has wheedled with his dissembling tongue. Your ladyship's own wisdom has been deluded by him; then how should I, a poor ignorant, defend myself ? O madam, if you knew but what he promised me, and how he assured me your ladyship should come to no damage ! Or else the wealth of the Indies should not have bribed me to conspire against so good, so sweet, so kind a lady as you have been to me.

30–31 cast servingman: dismissed servant
hospital: hospice, home for the destitute or sick
32 frontless: shameless
33 big-bellied actress: pregnant actress. Actresses did not have a good reputation.
36 void: invalid
38 consummated: completed the rites of marriage by sharing the bed
39 put upon his clergy: a criminal who could read and write could thereby claim 'benefit of clergy' and thus escape death sentence
40–41 meddle or make: cooperate in the plot
44 broker: marriage-broker or pimp; second-hand dealer
46 botcher: bungler, bad repairer
47 Abigails and Andrews: maidservants and menservants
47 baste: flog
48 Philander: lover
48 Duke's Place you: marry you in a hurried and irregular manner as was common at St James's Church in Duke's Place
51 parish: subdivision of county with its own church
53 Bridewell bride: a bride in the prison for women

LADY WISHFORT.

No damage? What, to betray me, to marry me to a cast servingman? to make me receptacle, an hospital for a decayed pimp? No damage? O thou frontless impudence, more than a big-bellied actress.

FOIBLE.

Pray do but hear me, madam; he could not marry your ladyship, madam. No indeed; his marriage was to have been void in law, for he was married to me first, to secure your ladyship. He could not have bedded your ladyship; for if he had consummated with your ladyship, he must have run the risk of the law and been put upon his clergy. Yes indeed; I inquired of the law in that case before I would meddle or make.

LADY WISHFORT.

What, then I have been your property, have I? I have been convenient to you, it seems! While you were catering for Mirabell, I have been broker for you? What, have you made a passive bawd of me? This exceeds all precedent; I am brought to fine uses, to become a botcher of secondhand marriages between Abigails and Andrews! I'll couple you! Yes, I'll baste you together, you and your Philander! I'll Duke's place you, as I'm a person! Your turtle is in custody already; you shall coo in the same cage, if there be constable or warrant in the parish. *Exit.*

FOIBLE.

Oh, that ever I was born! Oh that I was ever married! A bride! aye, I shall be a Bridewell-bride. Oh!

Enter Mrs. Fainall.

MRS. FAINALL.

Poor Foible, what's the matter?

FOIBLE.

O madam, my lady's gone for a constable. I shall be had to justice, and put to Bridewell to beat hemp. Poor Waitwell's gone to prison already.

62 missing effect: missing item of property or belonging
66 confederacy: conspiracy, alliance
68 stifled: suppressed
73ff The discovery of one secret amour—the Mirabell-Mrs Fainall affair—leads at once to the exposure of the marital infidelity of Fainall, his liaison with Mrs Marwood

MRS. FAINALL.

Have a good heart, Foible; Mirabell's gone to give security for him. This is all Marwood's and my huband's doing.

FOIBLE.

Yes, yes, I know it, madam; she was in my lady's closet, and overheard all that you said to me before dinner. She sent the letter to my lady; and that missing effect. Mr. Fainall laid this plot to arrest Waitwell, when he pretended to go for the papers; and in the meantime Mrs. Marwood declared all to my lady.

MRS. FAINALL.

Was there no mention made of me in the letter ? My mother does not suspect my being in the confederacy ? I fancy Marwood has not told her, though she has told my husband.

FOIBLE.

Yes, madam; but my lady did not see that part. We stifled the letter before she read so far. Has that mischievous devil told Mr. Fainall of your ladyship then?

MRS. FAINALL.

Aye, all's out, my affair with Mirabell, everything discovered. This is the last day of our living together; that's my comfort.

FOIBLE.

Indeed, madam, and so 'tis a comfort if you knew all. He has been even with your ladyship; which I could have told you long enough since, but I love to keep peace and quietness by my goodwill. I had rather bring friends together than set 'em at distance. But Mrs. Marwood and he are nearer related than ever their parents thought for.

MRS. FAINALL.

Say'st thou so, Foible? Canst thou prove this?

FOIBLE.

I can take my oath of it, madam; so can Mrs. Mincing. We have had many a fair word from Madam Marwood, to conceal something that passed in our chamber one evening when you were at Hyde Park and we were thought to have gone a-walking; but we went up unawares, though we were sworn to

90 My lady: Millamant

92–93 my old lady's: Lady Wishfort's

90–97 Mincing performs a valuable choric role, helping the audience pick up the love threads of a complicated plot reaching its climax. The intermeshing of property and passion is also brought to the fore.

secrecy too. Madam Marwood took a book and swore us upon it, but it was a book of verses and poems. So as long as it was not a Bible oath, we may break it with a safe conscience.

MRS. FAINALL.

This discovery is the most opportune thing I could wish. Now, Mincing?

Enter Mincing.

MINCING.

My lady would speak with Mrs. Foible, mem. Mr. Mirabell is with her; he has set your spouse at liberty, Mrs. Foible, and would have you hide yourself in my lady's closet till my old lady's anger is abated. Oh, my old lady is in a perilous passion at something Mr. Fainall has said; he swears, and my old lady cries. There's a fearful hurricane, I vow. He says, mem, how that he'll have my lady's fortune made over to him, or he'll be divorced.

MRS. FAINALL.

Does your lady or Mirabell know that?

MINCING.

Yes, mem; they have sent me to see if Sir Wilfull be sober and to bring him to them. My lady is resolved to have him, I think, rather than lose such a vast sum as six thousand pound. Oh, come, Mrs. Foible, I hear my old lady.

MRS. FAINALL.

Foible, you must tell Mincing that she must prepare to vouch when I call her.

FOIBLE.

Yes, yes, madam.

MINCING.

O yes, mem, I'll vouch anything for your ladyship's service, be what it will. *Exeunt* Mincing *and* Foible.

111 intercessor: one who intervenes or mediates

113 compound: settle matter by mutual concession

115–117 The travesty of obsolete pastoralism – which involved a fashionable rejection of urban society—is not unrelated to the sociable and urban basis of Restoration comedy. Lady Wishfort's planned retirement to a pastoral idyllic world is symptomatic of an affectation.

116 purling streams: streams flowing with whirling motion and babbling sound

118 dispatch: dispose of, settle

120 treaty: agreement

122 bone … flesh: Lady Wishfort pompously imitates Biblical language

129 naught: naughty

130 sophisticated: become false by losing natural innocence

132 plate: household utensils of silver, gold and so on

Enter Lady Wishfort *and* Marwood.

LADY WISHFORT.

O my dear friend, how can I enumerate the benefits that I have received from goodness? To you I owe the timely discovery of the false vows of Mirabell; to you the detection of the imposter Sir Rowland. And now you are become an intercessor with my son-in-law, to save the honour of my house, and compound for the frailties of my daughter. Well, friend, you are enough to reconcile me to the bad world, or else I would retire to deserts and solitudes, and feed harmless sheep by groves and purling streams. Dear Marwood, let us leave the world, and retire by ourselves and be shepherdesses.

MRS. MARWOOD.

Let us first dispatch the affair in hand, madam. We shall have leisure to think of retirement afterwards. Here is one who is concerned in the treaty.

LADY WISHFORT.

O daughter, daughter, is it possible thou shouldst be my child, bone of my bone, and flesh of my flesh, and, as I may say, another me, and yet transgress the most minute particle of severe virtue? It is possible you should lean aside to iniquity, who have been cast in the direct mould of virtue? I have not only been a mould but a pattern for you, and model for you, after you were brought into the world.

MRS. FAINALL.

I don't understand your ladyship.

LADY WISHFORT.

Not understand? Why, have you not been naught? Have you not been sophisticated? Not understand? Here I am ruined to compound for your caprices and your cuckoldoms. I must pawn my plate and my jewels, and ruin my niece, and all little enough.

MRS. FAINALL.

I am wronged and abused, and so are you. 'Tis a false accusation, as false as hell, as false as your friend there, aye, or your friend's friend, my false husband.

141 temper: moderation, restraint
151 destitute in this perplexity: helpless in this confusion
152 genius: guiding or tutelary spirit
155 bodkin: long hairpin
155 brass counter: coin of inferior metal and therefore of little value
157 stand by: stand up to
159ff Mrs Fainall's upbringing is yet another hilarious exercise in hypocrisy: her mother's puritanical suspicion of male company betrays an obsession with men and not unexpectedly reverses the intended effect
161 unexceptionable: with which no fault can be found
164 odium: strong dislike

MRS. MARWOOD.

My friend, Mrs. Fainall? Your husband my friend? What do you mean?

MRS. FAINALL.

I know what I mean, madam, and so do you; and so shall the world at a time convenient.

MRS. MARWOOD.

I am sorry to see you so passionate, madam. More temper would look more like innocence. But I have done. I am sorry my zeal to serve your ladyship and family should admit of misconstruction, or make me liable to affronts. You will pardon me, madam, if I meddle no more with an affair in which I am not personally concerned.

LADY WISHFORT.

O dear friend, I am so ashamed that you should meet with such returns ! [*To Mrs. Fainall.*] You ought to ask pardon on your knees, ungrateful creature; she deserves more from you than all your life can accomplish. [*To Mrs. Marwood.*] Oh, don't leave me destitute in this perplexity ! No, stick to me, my good genius.

MRS. FAINALL.

I tell you, madam, you're abused. Stick to you? Aye, like leech, to suck your best blood; she'll drop off when she's full. Madam, you shan't pawn a bodkin, nor part with a brass counter, in composition for me. I defy 'em all. Let 'em prove their aspersions; I know my own innocence, and dare stand by a trial.

Exit.

LADY WISHFORT.

Why, if she should be innocent, if she should be wronged after all, ha? I don't know what to think—and, I promise you, her education has been unexceptionable. I may say it; for I chiefly made it my own care to initiate her very infancy in the rudiments of virtue, and to impress upon her tender years a young odium and aversion to the very sight of men—aye, friend, she would ha' shrieked if she had but seen a man, till

168 babies: dolls, playthings

170 made ... her: ie, we managed to put up a pretence that the chaplain was a woman

171 sleek: smooth, soft and glossy

175 catechised: given religious instruction by a method of question and answer

177 lewd: indecent

179 swooned: fainted

182 excommunication: cutting off (as punishment) a person from all communication with the Church

185ff Mrs Marwood's advice to Lady Wishfort to avoid publicity presupposes an infrastructure of scandal including the press, the hawkers, the conventicles and the law-courts

186 worried: examined, probed

187 bawling: speaking noisily

188 *Oyez*: a cry uttered usually thrice by public crier or court officer to enforce silence

189 fumbling lecher: a groping, debauched person
quoif: a white cap worn by barristers
midwife: assistant during childbirth

190–91 legal ... statute: lawyers who will play upon words (pun and quibble) in an evasive or equivocal manner

193 Doomsday Book: ie, *Domesday Book*, a record of William the Conqueror's survey of the lands of England in 1086

194 interrogatories: questions

196 simpers: smiles affectedly, smirks, leers

196 fidges: fidgets

197 cantharides: dried Spanish flies used for aphrodisiac and diuretic purposes
cow-itch: cowhage, a tropical plant with stinging hairs on its pod

she was in her teens. As I'm a person, 'tis true. She was never suffered to play with a male child, though but in coats; nay, her very babies were of the feminine gender. Oh, she never looked a man in the face but her own father, or the chaplain, and him we made a shift to put upon her for a woman, by the help of his long garments and his sleek face, till she was going in her fifteen.

MRS. MARWOOD.

'Twas much she should be deceived so long.

LADY WISHFORT.

I warrant you, or she would never have borne to have been catechised by him; and have heard his long lectures against singing and dancing, and such debaucheries; and going filthy plays, and profane music-meetings, where the lewd trebles squeak nothing but bawdy, and the basses roar blasphemy. Oh, she would have swooned at the sight or name of an obscene playbook! And can I think, after all this, that my daughter can be naught? What, a whore? And thought it excommunication to set her foot within the door of a playhouse. O my dear friend, I can't believe it, no, no! As she says, let him prove it, let him prove it.

MRS. MARWOOD.

Prove it, madam? What, and have your name prostituted in a public court! Yours and your daughter's reputation worried at the bar by a pack of bawling lawyers! To be ushered in with an *Oyez* of scandal, and have your case opened by an old fumbling lecher in a quoif like a man midwife; to bring your daughter's infamy to light; to be a theme for legal punsters and quibblers by the statute, and become a jest against a rule of court, where there is no precedent for a jest in any record, not even in Doomsday Book; to discompose the gravity of the bench, and provoke naughty interrogatories in more naughty law Latin, while the good judge, tickled with the proceeding, simpers under a grey beard, and fidges off and on his cushion as if he had swallowed cantharides, or sat upon cow-itch.

200 revellers of the Temple: law students

201 take notes … conventicle: apprentices took notes on sermons for their dissenting masters

202 in commons: in the dining-hall

208 the flounder-man's: referring to the loud cry of street vendors selling flounders (small flat fish) on the streets of London

211 insupportable: unbearable

215 overseen: overlooked

221ff Fainall couches his blackmail in legal, contractual language which is so central to the world of the play, concerned as it is with the relationship of love and money In his confrontation with Sir Wilfull we glimpse an alternative language, but he is defeated only by the superior legal acumen and foresight of Mirabell. Behind all this, no doubt Congreve's legal training is at work, but surely the determining role of contracts in human relationships points to the emergent bourgeois ideology. If Mirabell wants Millamant it is not at the cost of the legacy, and the action of the play revolves round his strategy for acquiring the latter.

LADY WISHFORT.

Oh, 'tis very hard!

MRS. MARWOOD.

And then to have my young revellers of the Temple take notes, like prentices at a conventicle; and after, talk it all over again in commons, or before drawers in an eating house.

LADY WISHFORT.

Worse and worse!

MRS. MARWOOD.

Nay, this is nothing; if it would end here, 'twere well. But it must, after this, be consigned by the shorthand writers to the public press; and from thence be transferred to the hands, nay into the throats and lungs of hawkers, with voices more licentious than the loud flounder-man's, or the woman that cries grey peas. And this you must hear till you are stunned; nay, you must hear nothing else for some days.

LADY WISHFORT.

Oh, 'tis insupportable! No, no dear friend; make it up, make it up; aye, aye, I'll compound. I'll give up all, myself and my all, my niece and her all, anything, everything for composition.

MRS. MARWOOD.

Nay, madam. I advise nothing; I only lay before you, as a friend, the inconveniences which perhaps you have overseen. Here comes Mr. Fainall. If he will be satisfied to huddle up all in silence, I shall be glad. You must think I would rather congratulate than condole with you.

Enter Fainall.

LADY WISHFORT.

Aye, aye, I do not doubt it, dear Marwood; no, no, I do not doubt it.

FAINALL.

Well, madam, I have suffered myself to be overcome by the importunity of this lady your friend, and am content that you shall enjoy your own proper estate during life, on condition

237 physic: art of healing
238 apothecary: chemist
242 Muscovite husband: Russian husbands were considered to be barbaric on the basis of Elizabethan travellers' accounts.
243 Czarish majesty's retinue: the team of attendants with Peter the Great, the Russian Czar who had visited England in 1697.

you oblige yourself never to marry, under such penalty as I think convenient.

LADY WISHFORT.

Never to marry?

FAINALL.

No more Sir Rowlands; the next imposture may not be so timely detected.

MRS. MARWOOD.

That condition, I dare answer, my lady will consent to, without difficulty; she has already but too much experienced the perfidiousness of men. Besides madam, when we retire to our pastoral solitude, we shall bid adieu to all other thoughts.

LADY WISHFORT.

Aye, that's true; but in case of necessity, as of health, or some such emergency—

FAINALL.

Oh, if you are prescribed marriage, you shall be considered; I will only reserve to myself the power to choose for you. If your physic be wholesome, it matters not who is your apothecary. Next, my wife shall settle on me the remainder of her fortune, not made over already; and for her maintenance depend entirely on my discretion.

LADY WISHFORT.

This is most inhumanly savage, exceeding the barbarity of a Muscovite husband.

FAINALL.

I learned it from his Czarish majesty's retinue, in a winter evening's conference over brandy and pepper, amongst other secrets of matrimony and policy, as they are at present practised in the northern hemisphere. But this must be agreed unto, and that positively. Lastly, I will be endowed, in right of my wife, with that six thousand pound, which is the moiety of Mrs. Millamant's fortune in your possession; and which she has forfeited (as will appear by the last will and testament of your deceased husband, Sir Jonathan Wishfort) by her

256 *non compos*: not in his right mind
259 while … drawing: while the legal document is being prepared
260 more sufficient deeds: more satisfactory agreements
269 her year: her year of mourning the death of her husband
272 with a witness: i.e., she has met her match
273 confiscated: dispossessed, deprived
273–74 rebel rate: extortionate rate, high-handed manner
274 Egyptian plagues: Biblical allusion to the ten plagues in Exodus 7–12.

disobedience in contracting herself against your consent or knowledge, and by refusing the offered match with Sir Wilfull Witwoud, which you, like a careful aunt, had provided for her.

LADY WISHFORT.
My nephew was *non compos*, and could not make his addresses.

FAINALL.
I come to make demands. I'll hear no objections.

LADY WISHFORT.
You will grant me time to consider?

FAINALL.
Yes, while the instrument is drawing, to which you must set your hand till more sufficient deeds can be perfected; which I will take care shall be done with all possible speed. In the meanwhile, I will go for the said instrument, and till my return you may balance this matter in your own discretion. *Exit.*

LADY WISHFORT.
This insolence is beyond all precedent, all parallel. Must I be subject to this merciless villain?

MRS. MARWOOD.
'Tis severe indeed, madam, that you should smart for your daughter's wantonness.

LADY WISHFORT.
'Twas against my consent that she married this barbarian, but she would have him, though her year was not out. —Ah! her first husband, my son Languish, would not have carried it thus. Well, that was my choice, this is hers; she is matched now with a witness. I shall be mad! Dear friend, is there no comfort for me? Must I live to be confiscated at this rebel rate? —Here come two more of my Egyptian plagues, too.

Enter Millamant *and* Sir Wilfull Witwoud.

SIR WILFULL.
Aunt, your servant.

276 caterpillar: worthless fellow, parasite
277 in disguise: drunk
286 sacrifice to your repose: sacrifice myself for your peace of mind
297 Gorgon: (Greek mythology) one of three snake-haired women (especially Medusa) whose terrible looks turned any beholder to stone.

LADY WISHFORT.

Out, caterpillar, call me not aunt! I know thee not!

SIR WILFULL.

I confess I have been a little in disguise, as they say. 'Sheart! and I'm sorry for't. What would you have? I hope I committed no offence, aunt, and, if I did, I am willing to make satisfaction; and what can a man say fairer? If I have broke anything, I'll pay for't, an it cost a pound. And so let that content for what's past, and make no more words. For what's to come, to pleasure you. I'm willing to marry my cousin. So pray let's all be friends; she and I are agreed upon the matter before a witness.

LADY WISHFORT.

How's this, dear niece? Have I any comfort? Can this be true?

MILLAMANT.

I am content to be a sacrifice to your repose, madam; and to convince you that I had no hand in the plot, as you were misinformed, I have laid my commands on Mirabell to come in person, and be a witness that I give my hand to this flower of knighthood; and for the contract that passed between Mirabell and me, I have obliged him to make a resignation of it in your ladyship's presence. He is without, and waits your leave for admittance.

LADY WISHFORT.

Well, I'll swear I am something revived at this testimony of your obedience; but I cannot admit that traitor. I fear I cannot fortify myself to support his appearance. He is as terrible to me as a Gorgon; if I see him, I fear I shall turn to stone, petrify incessantly.

MILLAMANT.

If you disoblige him, he may resent your refusal and insist upon the contract still. Then 'tis the last time he will be offensive to you.

LADY WISHFORT.

Are you sure it will be the last time? If I were sure of that! Shall I never see him again?

307 Pylades and Orestes: famous friends and travelling companions in Greek mythology
309 proviso: condition
312–13 True to her nature, Mrs Marwood smells a plot improvised within a plot.
320 mum: silence
321–29 By skilfully parodying the stilted and outmodel language of courtly love, Mirabell prepares the ground for a different kind of love with its appropriate language.

MILLAMANT.

Sir Willfull, you and he are to travel together, are you not?

SIR WILFULL.

'Sheart, the gentleman's a civil gentleman, aunt; let him come in. Why, we are sworn brothers and fellow travellers. We are to be Pylades and Orestes, he and I. He is to be my interpreter in foreign parts. He has been overseas once already; and with proviso that I marry my cousin, will cross 'em once again, only to bear me company. 'Sheart, I'll call him in. An I set on't once, he shall come in; and see who'll hinder him *Exit.*

MRS. MARWOOD.

This is precious fooling, if it would pass; but I'll know the bottom of it.

LADY WISHFORT.

O dear Marwood, you are not going?

MRS. MARWOOD.

Not far, madam; I'll return immediately. *Exit.*

Re-enter Sir Wilfull *and* Mirabell.

SIR WILFULL.

Look up, man, I'll stand by you; 'sbud an she do frown, she can't kill you; besides—harkee, she dare not frown desperately, because her face is none of her own. 'Sheart, an she should, her forehead would wrinkle like the coat of a cream cheese; but mum for that, fellow traveller.

MIRABELL.

If a deep sense of the many injuries I have offered to so good a lady, with a sincere remorse and a hearty contrition, can but obtain the least glance of compassion, I am too happy. Ah, madam, there was a time ! But let it be forgotten. I confess I have deservedly forfeited the high place I once held, of sighing at your feet. Nay, kill me not, by turning from me in disdain. I come not to plead for favour; nay, not for pardon. I am a suppliant only for your pity. I am going where I never shall behold you more.

333 By'r Lady: By Our Lady
337 prejudice: harm, injury
340 venial: pardonable
344–45 o' the quorum: a Justice of the Peace
348 mouth-glue: a verbal promise and hence not legally binding

SIR WILFULL.

How, fellow traveller! You shall go by yourself then.

MIRABELL.

Let me be pitied first, and afterwards forgotten—I ask no more.

SIR WILFULL.

By'r Lady, a very reasonable request, and will cost you nothing, aunt. Come, come, forgive and forget, aunt; why you must, an you are a Christian.

MIRABELL.

Consider, madam, in reality you could not receive much prejudice; it was an innocent device, though I confess it had a face of guiltiness. It was at most an artifice which love contrived, and errors which love produces have ever been accounted venial. At least think it is punishment enough that I have lost what in my heart I hold most dear, that to your cruel indignation I have offered up this beauty, and with her my peace and quiet; nay, all my hopes of future comfort.

SIR WILFULL.

An he does not move me, would I might never be o'the quorum! An it were not as good a deed as to drink, to give her to him again, I would I might never take shipping! Aunt, if you don't forgive quickly, I shall melt, I can tell you that. My contract went no farther than a little mouth-glue, and that's hardly dry; one doleful sigh more from my fellow traveller, and 'tis dissolved.

LADY WISHFORT

Well, nephew, upon your account—ah, he has a false insinuating tongue! Well, sir, I will stifle my just resentment at my nephew's request. I will endeavour what I can to forget, but on proviso that you resign the contract with my niece immediately.

MIRABELL.

It is in writing and with papers of concern; but I have sent my servant for it, and will deliver it to you, with all acknowledgements for your transcendent goodness.

363 date of deliberation: period given to consider
371 pretensious: claims
374 fox: sword
375 instrument of ram vellum: legal document written on fine parchment made usually from calfskin
376 mittimus: warrant committing person to prison
tailor's measure: parchment strip used by tailors to take measurements
379 respite: defer

LADY WISHFORT [*aside*].

Oh, he has witchcraft in his eyes and tongue! When I did not see him, I could have bribed a villain to his assassination; but his appearance rakes the embers which have so long lain smothered in my breast.

Enter Fainall *and* Mrs. Marwood.

FAINALL.

Your date of deliberation, madam, is expired. Here is the instrument; are you prepared to sign?

LADY WISHFORT.

If I were prepared, I am not empowered. My niece exerts a lawful claim, having matched herself by my direction to Sir Wilfull.

FAINALL.

That sham is too gross to pass on me, though 'tis imposed on you, madam.

MILLAMANT.

Sir, I have given my consent.

MIRABELL.

And, sir, I have resigned my pretensions.

SIR WILFULL.

And, sir, I assert my right; and will maintain it in defiance of you, sir, and of your instrument. 'Sheart, an you talk of an instrument, sir, I have an old fox by my thigh. Shall hack your instrument of ram vellum to shreads, sir! It shall not be sufficient for mittimus or a tailor's measure. Therefore, withdraw your instrument, sir, or by'r Lady, I shall draw mine.

LADY WISHFORT.

Hold, nephew, hold!

MILLAMANT.

Good Sir Wilfull, respite your valour.

380 beefeater: yeoman of the Royal Guard. There is perhaps a caustic reference to Sir Wilfull's corpulence

383–84 pursuant … tenor: conforming to the meaning and direction

388 bear-garden: scene of tumult (derived from the sport of bear-baiting) Fainall compares Wilfull's behaviour to the violence and disorder of this sport

391 leaky hulk: leaking ship or boat

FAINALL.

Indeed? Are you provided of a guard, with your single beefeater there? But I'm prepared for you, and insist upon my first proposal. You shall submit your own estate to my management and absolutely make over my wife's to my sole use, as pursuant to the purport and tenor of this other covenant. [*To* Millamant.] I suppose, madam, your consent is not requisite in this case; nor, Mr. Mirabell, your resignation; nor, Sir Wilfull, your right. You may draw your fox if your please, sir, and make a bear-garden flourish somewhere else, for here it will not avail. This, my Lady Wishfort, must be subscribed, or your darling daughter's turned adrift, like a leaky hulk, to sink or swim, as she and the current of this lewd town can agree.

LADY WISHFORT.

Is there no means, no remedy to stop my ruin? Ungrateful wretch! dost thou not owe thy being, thy subsistence, to my daughter's fortune?

FAINALL.

I'll answer you when I have the rest of it in my possession.

MIRABELL.

But that you would not accept of a remedy from my hands—I own I have not deserved you should owe any obligation to me; or else perhaps I could advise—

LADY WISHFORT.

Oh, what? what? to save me and my child from ruin, from want I'll forgive all that's past; nay I'll consent to anything to come, to be delivered from this tyranny.

MIRABELL.

Aye, madam, but that is too late; my reward is intercepted. You have disposed of her who only could have made me a compensation for all my services. But be it as it may, I am resolved I'll serve you; you shall not be wronged in this savage manner.

418ff The explosion of hatred, malice and ill-feeling in this entire scene contrasts oddly with the elegant veneer – it is the underbelly of modish, rakish wit.

420 tittle: bit

LADY WISHFORT.

How! Dear Mr. Mirabell, can you be so generous at last? But it is not possible. Harkee, I'll break my nephew's match; you shall have my niece yet, and all her fortune, if you can but save me from this imminent danger.

MIRABELL.

Will you? I take you at your word. I ask no more. I must have leave for two criminals to appear.

LADY WISHFORT.

Aye, aye; anybody, anybody!

MIRABELL.

Foible is one, and a penitent.

Enter Mrs. Fainall, Foible, *and* Mincing.

MRS. MARWOOD [*to* Fainall].

Oh, my shame! These corrupt things are bought and brought hither to expose me.

Mirabell *and* Lady Wishfort *go to* Mrs. Fainall *and* Foible.

FAINALL.

If it must all come out, why let'em know it; 'tis but the way of the world. That shall not urge me to relinquish or abate one tittle of my terms; no, I will insist the more.

FOIBLE.

Yes indeed, madam; I'll take my Bible oath of it.

MINCING.

And so will I, mem.

LADY WISHFORT.

O Marwood, Marwood, art thou false? my friend deceive me? Hast thou been a wicked accomplice with that profligate man?

MRS. MARWOOD.

Have you so much ingratitude and injustice, to give credit against your friend to the aspersions of two such mercenary trulls?

429 garret: attic, room under an arched roof

430 Messalina: licentious wife of the Roman emperor Claudius, but she did not write poetry Mincing probably means 'miscellaneous'

434 expedient: trick, device

438 aspersed: slandered, accused

441 groat: English silver coin worth four pence (issued 1351–1662)

MINCING.

Mercenary, mem? I scorn your words. 'Tis true we found you and Mr. Fainall in the blue garret; by the same token, you swore us to secrecy upon Messalina's poems. Mercenary? No, if we would have been mercenary, we should have held our tongues; you would have bribed us sufficiently.

FAINALL.

Go, you are an insignificant thing! Well, what are you the better for this? Is this Mr. Mirabell's expedient? I'll be put off no longer. You thing, that was a wife, shall smart for this! I will not leave thee wherewithal to hide thy shame; your body shall be as naked as your reputation.

MRS. FAINALL.

I despise you, and defy your malice! You have aspersed me wrongfully. I have proved your falsehood. Go you and your treacherous—I will not name it, but starve together, perish!

FAINALL.

Not while you are worth a groat, indeed, my dear. Madam, I'll be fooled no longer.

LADY WISHFORT.

Ah, Mr. Mirabell, this is small comfort, the detection of this affair.

MIRABELL.

Oh, in good time. Your leave for the other offender and penitent to appear, madam.

Enter Waitwell *with a box of writings.*

LADY WISHFORT.

O Sir Rowland! Well, rascal?

WAITWELL.

What your ladyship pleases. I have brought the black box at last, madam.

MIRABELL.

Give it to me. Madam, you remember your promise.

455 Whose hand's out?: more or less the same as 'What's the matter'?

456 Heyday!: interjection expressing joy or surprise

461 You wrong him: As usual Witwoud tries to act superior by suggesting that Petulant cannot sign his name, but this time Mirabell rebuts him bluntly.

LADY WISHFORT.
Aye, dear sir.

MIRABELL.
Where are the gentlemen?

WAITWELL.
At hand, sir, rubbing their eyes; just risen from sleep.

FAINALL.
'Sdeath, what's this to me? I'll not wait your private concerns.

Enter Petulant *and* Witwoud.

PETULANT.
How now? What's the matter? Whose hand's out?

WITWOUD.
Heyday! what, are you all got together, like players at the end of the last act?

MIRABELL.
You may remember, gentlemen, I once requested your hands as witnesses to a certain parchment.

WITWOUD.
Aye, I do; my hand I remember. Petulant set his mark.

MIRABELL.
You wrong him; his name is fairly written, as shall appear. You do not remember, gentlemen, anything of what that parchment contained? *Undoing the box.*

WITWOUD.
No.

PETULANT.
Not I. I writ. I read nothing.

MIRABELL.
Very well; now you shall know. Madam, your promise.

LADY WISHFORT.
Aye, aye, sir upon my honour.

482	occasions:affairs or business (especially legal)
484	conveyance: the written instrument for legal transference of real property estate real: lands and estates, immovable property
486	the way of the world: An ironic echo of Fainall's unscrupulous interpretation of the credo in lines 418–19.
487	elder: earlier
490	bear-garden: Similar echo of Fainall's words in line 388.
492–93	Fainall's unrepentant and unabashed viciousness, may recall the character of Tartuffe in Molire's comedy *Tartuffe*.

MIRABELL.

Mr. Fainall, it is now time that you should know that your lady, while she was at her own disposal, and before you had by your insinuations wheedled her out of a pretended settlement of the greatest part of her fortune—

FAINALL.

Sir! pretended!

MIRABELL.

Yes, sir. I say that this lady, while a widow, having, it seems, received some cautions respecting your inconstancy and tyranny of temper, which from her own partial opinion and fondness of you she could never have suspected—she did, I say, by the wholesome advice of friends and of sages learned in the laws of this land, deliver this same as her act and deed to me in trust, and to the uses within mentioned. You may read if you please [*Holding out the parchment.*]—though perhaps what is inscribed on the back may serve your occasions.

FAINALL.

Very likely, sir. What's here? Damnation ! [*Reads.*] "A deed of conveyance of the whole estate real of Arabella Languish, widow, in trust to Edward Mirabell." Confusion!

MIRABELL.

Even so, sir; 'tis the way of the world, sir, of the widows of the world. I suppose this deed may bear an elder date than what you have obtained from your lady.

FAINALL.

Perfidious fiend! then thus I'll be revenged.

Offers to run at Mrs. Fainall.

SIR WILFULL.

Hold sir! Now you may make your bear-garden flourish somewhere else, sir.

FAINALL.

Mirabell, you shall hear of this, sir; be sure you shall. Let me pass, oaf! *Exit.*

488–99 Lady Wishfort's claim is absurd because there is little similarity between mother and daughter. The absurdity, however, restores the tone of the comedy.

509 prosecute: pursue

515 off or on: Petulant shows he does not really care.

516 I gad: *by God*

MRS. FAINALL.

Madam, you seem to stifle your resentment; you had better give it vent.

MRS. MARWOOD.

Yes, it shall have vent, and to your confusion; or I'll perish in the attempt. *Exit.*

LADY WISHFORT.

O daughter, daughter, 'tis plain thou hast inherited thy mother's prudence.

MRS. FAINALL.

Thank Mr. Mirabell, a cautious friend, to whose advice all is owing.

LADY WISHFORT.

Well, Mr. Mirabell, you have kept your promise, and I must perform mine. First, I pardon, for your sake, Sir Rowland there and Foible. The next thing is to break the matter to my nephew, and how to do that—

MIRABELL.

For that, madam, give yourself no trouble, let me have your consent. Sir Wilful is my friend; he has had compassion upon lovers, and generously engaged a volunteer in this action for our service, and now designs to prosecute his travels.

SIR WILFULL.

'Sheart, aunt, I have no mind to marry. My cousin's a fine lady, and the gentleman loves her, and she loves him, and they deserve one another; my resolution is to see foreign parts. I have set on't, and when I'm set on't, I must do't. And if these two gentlemen would travel too, I think they may be spared.

PETULANT.

For my part, I say little; I think things are best off or on.

WITWOUD.

I gad, I understand nothing of the matter; I'm in a maze yet, like a dog in a dancing school.

525 toy: play, embrace

526 dance: A familiar stage ritual of joyous harmony, often related to marriage in comedy.

LADY WISHFORT.

Well, sir, take her, and with her all the joy I can give you.

MILLAMANT.

Why does not the man take me? Would you have me give myself to you over again?

MIRABELL.

Aye, and over and over again; for I would have you as often as possibly I can. [*Kisses her hand*] Well, heaven grant I love you not too well; that's all my fear.

SIR WILFULL.

'Sheart, you'll have time enough to toy after you're married; or if you will toy now, let us have a dance in the meantime, that we who are not lovers may have some other employment besides looking on.

MIRABELL.

With all my heart, dear Sir Wilfull. What shall we do for music?

FOIBLE.

Oh, sir, some that were provided for Sir Rowland's entertainment are yet within call.

A dance.

LADY WISHFORT.

As I am a person, I can hold out no longer. I have wasted my spirits so today already that I am ready to sink under the fatigue; and I cannot but have some fears upon me yet that my son Fainall will pursue some desperate course.

MIRABELL.

Madam, disquiet not yourself on that account; to my knowledge his circumstances are such, he must of force comply. For my part, I will contribute all that in me lies to reunion. In the meantime, madam [*To* Mrs. Fainall.], let me before these witnesses restore to you this deed of

542 means: Fainall will be brought back to his wife and the marital arrangement (without which a woman had no status in society) will be kept up because of the legacy—that has the last word.

trust; it may be a means, well-managed, to make you live easily together.

From hence let those be warned, who mean to wed,
Lest mutual falsehood stain the bridal bed;
For each deceiver to his cost may find,
That marriage frauds too oft are paid in kind.

Exeunt omnes.

3 doom: condemn

11 pit: that part of a theatre auditorium which is on the floor just below the stage

17 scurrilous: grossly or obscenely abusive

21 glosses: explanatory notes (eg glossary)

22 libel: false, defamatory statement

30 abstracted: selected from many

36 *belles assemblées*: fashionable company

coquettes: women who play with male attentions and affections

beaux: fops, dandies

EPILOGUE

Spoken by Mrs. Bracegirdle

After our Epilogue this crowd dismisses,
I'm thinking how this play'll be pulled to pieces.
But pray consider, ere you doom its fall,
How hard a thing 'twould be to please you all.
There are some critics so with spleen diseased,
They scarcely come inclining to be pleased;
And sure he must have more than mortal skill;
Who pleases any one against his will.
Then, all bad poets we are sure are foes,
And how their number's swelled, the town well knows;
In shoals I've marked 'em judging in the pit;
Though they're on no pretense for judgment fit,
But that they have been damned for want of wit.
Since when, they, by their own offences taught,
Set up for spies on plays, and finding fault.
Others there are whose malice we'd prevent;
Such who watch plays with scurrilous intent
To mark out who by characters are meant.
And though no perfect likeness they can trace,
Yet each pretends to know the copied face.
These with false glosses feed their own ill nature,
And turn to libel what was meant a satire.
May such malicious fops this fortune find,
To think themselves alone the fools designed;
If any are so arrogantly vain,
To think they singly can support a scene,
And furnish fool enough to entertain.
For well the learned and the judicious know
That satire scorns to stoop so meanly low
As any one abstracted fop to show.
For, as when painters form a matchless face,
They from each fair one catch some different grace;
And shining features in one portrait blend,
To which no single beauty must pretend;
So poets oft do in one piece expose
Whole *belles assemblées* of coquettes and beaux.

DISCUSSION TOPICS AND QUESTIONS

Given below are some topics to facilitate discussion, which are followed by questions based on the text.

Plot; themes; characters; comedy of manners; wit (false wit and true wit); affectation; sexual licence; the Proviso Scene; property (inheritance), law and marriage; women and gossip; women, the passing of beauty and old age; the black box; St James's Park, the chocolate house, town and country; servants

1. By focusing on manners, *The Way of the World* exposes the moral emptiness of upper-class Restoration society. Discuss.
2. The contrast between true wit and false wit in the play is not so much a linguistic issue as a social one. Discuss.
3. In *The Way of the World*, the socially mobile middle class aspires to aristocratic deportment and thus produces the widespread phenomenon of affectation. Discuss.
4. Is there a link between acquisitive greed and sexual licence in the play? Give a reasoned answer.
5. Marriage in *The Way of the World* is a hypocritical cover for sexual intrigue. Discuss.
6. In *The Way of the World,* marriage and courtship are inseparable from the pursuit of a legacy. Discuss.
7. The play shows women trapped in small talk, gossip and petty rivalries. Do you agree?
8. Without marriage, there is neither economic security nor respectability for women in *The Way of the World*. Discuss.
9. Despite their shared fate, women in the play largely have no sense of solidarity. Do you agree?
10. What effect does Congreve achieve by yoking lust to old age, as in the case of Lady Wishfort?
11. Is the black box a device suddenly thrust in to solve all problems or is it in consonance with the world of the play?
12. Show how, despite his boorishness, Sir Wilful Witwoud in *The Way of the World* offers a counterblast to so-called urban elegance.
13. What are the elements that contribute to the compact plot or structure of the play?

14. Do you think that the enclosed, inbred world of the play demands the tight plot construction that it is famous for?
15. The Millamant-Mirabell relationship reveals genuine passion in the guise of wit and coquetry. Discuss with special reference to the Proviso Scene.
16. The love of Millamant and Mirabell offers a critique of the conventions of courtship and marriage in upper-class Restoration society. Discuss.
17. Characters are often presented as contrasted and yet interlinked pairs in *The Way of the World.* Discuss with reference to Mirabell and Fainall, Mrs. Fainall and Mrs. Marwood and Witwoud and Petulant.
18. By participating in the milieu of intrigue and affectation, the servants in *The Way of the World* expose its hollowness. Do you agree?
19. How far is it correct to see Mirabell and Fainall as flip sides of the same coin?
20. Write a note on the setting—interior and exterior—of the play.

FURTHER READING

Birdsall, Virginia Ogden. *Wild Civility: The English Comic Spirit on the Restoration Stage.* Bloomington: Indiana University Press, 1970.

Brown, J.R. & Harris Bernard. *Restoration Theatre*: Stratford Upon Avon Studies 6. London: Edward Arnold, 1965.

Dobrée, Bonamy. *Restoration Comedy 1660–1720.* Oxford: The Clarendon Press, 1924.

Fujimura, Thomas H. *The Restoration Comedy of Wit.* Princeton, New Jersey: Princeton University Press, 1952.

Holland, Norman N. *The First Modern Comedies.* Cambridge, Massachusettes: Harvard University Press, 1959.

Kaul, A.N. *The Action of English Comedy.* New Haven: Yale University Press, 1970.

Knights, L.C. *Explorations.* London: Chatto & Windus, 1946.

Krutch, Joseph Wood. *Comedy and Conscience after the Restoration.* New York: Columbia University Press, 1949.

Loftis, John. *Comedy and Society from Congreve to Fielding.* Stanford: Stanford University Press, 1959.

Love, Harold. *Congreve.* Oxford: Basil Blackwell, 1974.

Lynch, Kathleen M. *The Social Mode of Restoration Comedy.* New York: MacMillan, 1926.

Mueschke, Paul & Miriam. *A New View of Congreve's The Way of the World.* Michigan: Folcroft Library Editions, 1958.

Muir, Kenneth. *The Comedy of Manners.* London: Prometheus Books 1970.

Nicoll, Allardyce. *A History of English Drama, 1660–1900.* Cambridge: Cambridge University Press, 1965.

Novak, Maximillian E. *William Congreve.* New York: Twayne Publishers, 1971.

Palmer, John. *The Comedy of Manners.* London: G. Bell & Sons, 1913.
Comedy. London: Russel & Russel, 1914.

Smith, John Harrington. *The Gay Couple in Restoration Comedy.* Cambridge, Massachusettes: Harvard University Press, 1948.

Voris, W.H. Van. *The Cultivated Stance: The Designs of Congreve's Plays.* Dublin: The Dolman Press, 1965.

Williams, Aubrey L. *An Approach to Congreve.* New Haven and London: Yale University Press, 1979.